DON'T PANIC

UNDERSTANDING PERSONAL DEBT

NICK LEESON

The
History
Press
Ireland

First published 2013

The History Press Ireland
50 City Quay
Dublin 2
Ireland
www.thehistorypress.ie

British Library Cataloguing in Publication Data.
A catalogue record for this book is available from the British Library.

ISBN 978 1 84588 808 4

Typesetting and origination by The History Press

Contents

About the Author

Nick Leeson became infamous in 1995 for his central role in the collapse of Barings Bank, which was dramatized in the film *Rogue Trader*. He was sentenced to six-and-a-half years in a Singaporean jail, during which time he was diagnosed with colon cancer. Since his release, Nick has now fully recovered from his illness, and currently lives in Galway with his wife, Leona. In 2006, he was appointed CEO of Galway United FC where he remained for five years. Nick is currently a Principal in GDP Partnership, where he endeavours to use his experience, both of economic risk and of personal adversity, to advise individuals and businesses in financial hardship.

1

How Did We Get Here?

It was evident from the general tone of the whole party,
that they had come to regard insolvency as the normal
state of mankind, and the payment of debts as a disease
that occasionally broke out.

Charles Dickens, *Little Dorrit*

I moved to Ireland in January 2003. At that time, Ireland was a land of unlimited opportunity, in which European Union money had kick-started a boom in the economy that could be seen everywhere you looked; huge improvements were being made to the infrastructure of the country, the Punt had recently been swapped for the Euro, interest rates were the lowest that they had ever been and falling further, and credit was available in abundance. There was a tangible sense that there was no end to the millions and a million ways to make them. And, of course, a lot of houses were being built. These factors combined to paint a picture of economic prosperity that was the envy of European nations. It sounds idyllic, and for many it was, but for each of those positives there was a negative lurking in the shadows.

Swapping the Punt for the Euro was, in retro-spect, the first step in losing control over fiscal responsibility and direction. Low interest rates convinced everyone that they had the time to pay and that it only made sense to borrow. And when you did apply for credit, it was so readily avail-able that the decision-making processes were not always as robust as they might have been.

The sum of those three situations was that the day of reckoning was never really far away. Nobody had any idea quite how calami-tous the sequence of events would prove to be, or how damaging the impact would become, but it was always coming. We have all learned that to our cost.

Recent revelations have also compounded the widely held suspicions that some bankers were reserving a particular brand of contempt for the governments and regulators. Bonus time was always going to come around, so leverage up or stay at home. This was a party, and it was never, ever going to stop.

That rings a chord with me, I have to admit. I was out of control during my time in Singapore. I was continually buying myself time, postponing the realisation of the losses that were mounting in my illegal trading account, but as long as I had access to money and funding for my illegal positions, I could keep going.

More money was always available. The bank I worked for, Barings, would find some way of arranging it as they believed, like many of us, that we were on a gravy train that knew no end. They felt that they had stumbled on a golden goose that was making money hand over fist in Singapore and, as a result, keeping me happy and trading was at the top of the agenda.

Very few questions were ever asked when the coffers ran dry. More money was borrowed from Barclays and Citibank, their principal lenders at that time. Money was coming from the Head Office in London and the treasury department of Barings, and was readily available as long as I reported a healthy profit. There was very little control.

Eventually, though, the bank did run out of money. Barings was, in the scheme of things, only a small bank. Its capital base of

£250 million was minimal in global banking terms, and by the end of 1994, the losses in my illegal account must have been getting close to £500 million, twice the capital base.

As long as the funds were available I kept going, in the increasingly forlorn hope that I would be able to turn the position around and get back to normality. From a high of 39,995, the Nikkei 225 Futures (the most widely used of the Japanese stock market indices) had fallen to half that value and the market was falling with increasing pace.

Barings' Head Office finally had no more money to send, and the banks that were lending to them to facilitate my positions in Singapore had closed shop, unwilling to loan any more. My number really should have been up at that stage but, rather than ask difficult questions, the bank looked for new ways to find money. They went to the stock market and issued a bond for £100 million, which went exactly the same way as the rest, which was into my illegal trading account and out through the losses that were ballooning out of control. Eventually all the money – Barings' own, the loans from Barclays and Citibank and any bondholders involved – was all hoovered up into the £862 million worth of losses, which ultimately signalled the collapse of the bank.

In part, the role played by the board and those responsible for running Barings bore similarities to those in charge at Anglo Irish Bank. They weren't really worried where the money was coming from as long as the bank was able to continue. Over time, the attempts to raise funds got more and more desperate. The similarities to the situation do not end there. Lending was sometimes reckless in the extreme, controls failed to function and were sometimes brazenly ignored, regular audits failed to highlight the problems and systems could be overridden when they needed to be.

The markets that I used to trade in are often described as complex. I suppose it is a matter of opinion but the activity that sparked the major problems in Ireland, lending, is as simple as can be. The parameters are tried and tested over hundreds of years and, if adhered to, they generally work. In Ireland, during the decade before the property crash, those parameters were breached time after time after time, with brutal consequences.

As everyone knows, the Irish economy expanded rapidly during the Celtic Tiger years of 1994–2007. In part this was due to a low corporate tax rate and low European Central Bank interest rates as mentioned, but there was another set of systemic factors that created anomalies in the way the Irish State was governed. These included an extremely soft surveillance of banking supervision against the Basel Core Principals adopted in most other European nations, and the adoption of poor policies such as a corporate tax system that fostered non-tradable goods and services through the construction industry. The credit expansion that this resulted in was unrivalled, which then fuelled the property bubble that followed. This, in turn, started to experience problems from 2007 onwards, and these problems gathered pace throughout the ensuing global financial crisis and reached its zenith in September 2008 on the night the infamous guarantee was put in place.

In the period from 2004–2008, Irish banks' foreign borrowings rose from €15 billion to €110 billion. The banks were lending long term to borrowers, principally the larger property developers, and borrowing themselves on a three-month roll-over basis. The properties that the loans were based upon would not typically be sold for several years so, when the property crisis hit and they could not be sold at all, due to massive over-supply and limited demand, the result was a classic mismatch of assets and liabilities. When government and banking officials met in September 2008 and decided to issue the bank guarantee, this was, of course, an attempt to stem the crisis and the hugely damaging uncertainty around the financial system. The banks were said to be illiquid (but not insolvent) by €4 billion. This turned out to be quite a significant underestimation.

The bill to bailout the banks was to eventually be astronomical.

Anglo Irish Bank was the first to fall. A boutique lender to builders and developers, the bank had made a succession of highly leveraged bets on the future of Ireland's increasingly unsustainable property market, and its spectacular collapse made it the poster child across the world for banking profligacy and short-sightedness. The eventual bill to the Irish taxpayer was reported to be in excess of €29 billion.

All of the banks, however, bore some responsibility for the size and scale of the crash. Irish Nationwide Building Society (INBS) had been a more traditional lender that morphed into a major player in the commercial property market. Many questions have been raised about the nature of the corporate oversight, practices and internal policies which ultimately allowed INBS to cost the State over €5 billion. Allied Irish Banks (AIB) and Bank of Ireland, the 'pillar banks' of the Irish economy, were both to receive €3.5 billion and AIB remains almost fully nationalised as a result.

How the mighty have fallen. From the peaks of the economic boom to the troughs that many of us are now facing, the contrast could not be starker. Before the recent banking meltdown in Cyprus, the Irish banking crisis was the most costly of modern times and accounted for about 40% of the country's GDP. The crisis will rank as one of the biggest banking failures in history, a stark example of poor regulation and an example of how banking, property and government that became far too closely entwined, compromising the fundamental principles of all three in the process.

By the end of 2007, the economy and the government finances were already showing signs of impending recession. Tax revenues were falling short of the annual budget forecast by €2.3 billion, and stamp duty and income tax fell short by €800 million. This resulted in the 2007 general government budget surplus being wiped out in a stroke. Winter was coming and mid-2008 government deficits had begun to snowball out of control, unemployment had increased and many businesses were being forced to close their doors. The Irish Stock Exchange Quotient (ISEQ) fell to its lowest level in years and migrant workers left in droves. Much of the native Irish workforce also began to look abroad, out of necessity. The acceleration into recession, and ultimately depression, was too much to take for many individuals, and the drain of some of the best Irish entrepreneurial minds from these shores continues.

The headline figures of the debt problem that have resulted are quite astounding. Approximately 180,000 home-loan and buy-to-let borrowers are now behind on their payments. By the end of March 2013, 12.3% of residential mortgages were three months or more in arrears and this figure is increasing quarter upon quarter. The rather more worrying figure is that almost 26,000 of these loans had been in arrears for over two years. And these figures are rising. These numbers, while staggering, are also not a surprise. They do, however, suggest both the extent of the problem and how much and how little is being done about it.

The government are now pinning a lot of the hope of recovery on the new Personal Insolvency Regime. It is hoped that it will help the country get a grip on the deep household and home-loans debt crisis that is stalling economic recovery. Part of that process will involve ensuring that the options available are very clearly understood and the most appropriate route for each individual is taken. The Insolvency Service of Ireland (ISI) becomes the centre piece of these new debt solution laws which will hopefully allow for the distressed borrower to reach a deal with their bank. The overriding ambition will be to provide a solution to all people with unsustainable debt and provide a platform whereby they can be restored to solvency from their current distressed position.

There is little point in beating around the bush on this matter. Ireland is facing one of the deepest personal financial debt crises anywhere in the world. In my opinion, the true extent of the problem remains only partially discovered. Many banks have effectively been sitting on their hands, waiting for something to happen. I've personally seen episodes where banks have allowed mortgages to go unpaid for as long as four years, which is hard to comprehend. As much as the borrowers have been putting their head in the sand, so, it seems, have the banks, hoping – like I did nearly two decades ago – that some Eureka moment would arrive and everything would correct itself. But it won't.

These problems are for the most part a legacy of the country's severe – and nearly fatal – banking and property ills, which forced Ireland to initially seek that bailout of €67.5 billion from the EU and IMF in late 2010. Widespread unemployment has been one of the immediate consequences, soaring to over 14% from a pre-crisis level of only 4%, a level that is accepted internationally as to be effectively full employment. Unemployment immediately compounds most problems, squeezing household incomes even further, leading to increased default on any number of credit agreements. Add austerity into this mix, with new taxes and a host of other charges, and it is easy to see how the problem has escalated so quickly.

When what follows is a squeeze on credit, the situation can become a stranglehold. This would traditionally have affected those described as 'working class' more significantly, but that is not the case here. This particular credit squeeze has gripped the whole country, and particularly the middle classes who have grown used to ready access to credit, and they are struggling.

The net result is that Ireland now has three classes of people: the wealthy and cash rich, who are seeing huge opportunity and getting quickly richer; a large number that are having to be exceptionally careful to keep themselves afloat; and a significant number of people who have already run out of money.

Unfortunately, the number that we see running out of money is escalating all the time and the only way to arrest this is to formulate a plan. The new Insolvency Regime will be, for many, the beginning of that process. The regime provides solutions for three types of debtors and includes a 'Debt Relief Notice' (DRN) for households with low income and few assets; a 'Debt Settlement Arrangement' (DSA) for unsecured debt; and a 'Personal Insolvency Arrangement' (PIA) for households with both secured and unsecured debt. The government will appoint six new judges to oversee the high volume of arrangements that will be required.

Widespread debt relief, in my opinion, was the solution but none of the Irish Banks had the capital base to withstand it, and that is probably why it has taken so long to reach this position. The process will start but it will continue to be gradual, which in itself is a reason to stay engaged with your bank and to keep them appraised of your situation. The Central Bank has now said that the banks have enough capital to deal with their customers but only on a 'case-by-case' basis and that the review will not lead to any widespread writing down of household debt by the lenders.

While much blame rests at the door of the nation's lenders, and it is important that we remember how this situation occurred so it is not repeated, the focus of this book is to look at the solutions that are available to you individually. As we all suffer and try to face debt square in the face, it is important to remember much of the problem may be someone else's doing, but there are things you can do to help yourself. Almost everyone is affected to some degree, and while debt may still be a word that is whispered in corners, it is touching more of us than you can imagine. Debt has become a subject of the mainstream, and it is time to look at the tools that will allow us to deal with it robustly, and finally move forward again.

2

The Five Emotional Stages of Debt

There are any number of events that can generate enormous stress. These can be as common and as superficially benign as moving house or changing school, or as life-altering as divorce and serious illness. I've often been quoted as saying that I have, unfortunately, experienced them all. In my own life I have been in the eye of several storms, and because of those times I believe I have learned some valuable lessons, which I hope might be of use to people in Ireland today. In particular, what I have noticed is that people no longer whisper the word 'cancer' like they used to. Due to increased communication, public discussion and better treatment, it has become something which can be talked about more openly, and this has, crucially, taken away some of the fear of the unknown.

Of course it is still serious, I can testify to that myself, but this increased openness has empowered people to seek treatment earlier, rather than bury their head in the sand, with often live-saving consequences. But what I've noticed is that another word seems to have replaced 'cancer' in this respect. It is, unfortunately, another issue which affects many of us, but yet retains a sense of stigma which leaves people isolated and afraid to address their problems, with often highly damaging results. And this word is 'debt'.

Because of the slightly murky connotations attached to the word, it can be very easy to feel that you are on your own. The last thing you want is for the neighbours or your friends to know, so the inclination is to keep quiet, to internalise what you are feeling and try to cope alone. If you are anything like me, you may fail in this, quite disastrously.

The overriding lesson from my forty-six years of experience, including the Barings saga and my own role in its collapse, was that things might have been different had I communicated better. If I asked more questions, asked for help or advice or simply told anybody about what was happening, things might have worked out very differently. I didn't however, and what I learned is that when you fail to engage, the situation only gets worse. Of course, in my case, the debt was larger than most, and peaked at £862 million and led to the fall of a bank. But the message is still the same. The more you understand the options available, the more you are able to engage with lenders and advisors, and the more positive the outcome will be. Ignoring problems has never yet made them go away.

Debt is nothing new to me. I was born into a very working-class family in Watford in 1967. We lived in a small flat throughout my early childhood, only moving to a council house on the outskirts of the city when my siblings were born. We never wanted for anything, and I used to go on all the school trips, even visiting America on an exchange programme. My mother would always make sure that we were well looked after and afforded every opportunity we possibly could have, especially if there was an educational benefit.

But there was always debt.

I didn't notice at the time, of course, but it was all around us. Our clothes were bought from a catalogue, and paid for over time; we had a television that required an endless stream of fifty pence pieces to keep it going. The 'Telly Man' would call by every week to collect his money, but I vividly remember my mother had found a way to relieve the television of its bounty and would feed them back into the TV to keep it going for us, so he was often not happy. She would be on the lookout for him, scanning the street for his arrival, and 'hiding from the Telly Man' became one of her favourite games, as we were all herded into the kitchen at the back of the house to pretend we were out.

Debt was, at that time, much like today, something that was hidden, vaguely embarrassing and certainly never spoken about. But the truth was we needed to talk about it, as do many people now. Many lives in Ireland have changed dramatically over recent years. Debt is life-altering, and as such, the way we deal with it goes through a number of distinct stages, which we will look at now.

Denial

Denial represents the first stage of dealing with any negative situation. There must be some mistake, this can't be happening to me. If I don't think about it, it will go away.

I was 31 years old when I was diagnosed with colon cancer. I was probably as fit as at any time in my life, exercising regularly, albeit within a prison regime in Singapore, and as slim as I'd been in a decade. I was, however, completely ignorant of the warning signs that were starting to mount. I hadn't touched an alcoholic drink in three and a half years but was suffering from dizzy spells when getting up from the floor. I had pains in my stomach that would not abate and, as much as I ate, I could never satiate the hunger. I was a glowing example of how to ignore everything and allow things to get worse.

After six months I finally went to the doctor, who diagnosed me as being anaemic. I was given some iron tablets. The pain hit a plateau, and while it wasn't getting any worse, neither was it getting any better. Eventually I realised that I had to take back control; as long as I was taking the iron tablets, in everybody else's opinion I was being treated. The very next day I refused the medication. This effectively handed the problem back to the prison doctor who eventually allowed me to go for a check-up at an outside hospital. In A&E the next morning, a lump was found, I was immediately admitted to the prison ward of the hospital and within eight days I had an emergency operation to remove one third of my colon. A six-month bout of chemotherapy followed, but I felt like I had taken back control. And, crucially, I was no longer in denial.

In financial terms, denial can creep in as the bills start to escalate. In the early days you might have made a few calls to lenders and tried to offer solutions. Typically, these initial targets can be overly optimistic, and people often quickly fall behind again.

Deep down, there might be a growing sense that the situation is slipping out of control. The temptation can be to bury your head in the sand at this point, and wait for the storm to pass. How you treat the post can be a telling sign. There are those who will have a look at the mail, see the bills and the letters from the bank, and quickly put them out of harm's way in the pile that is mounting on a shelf. There are those who read the letters, before ripping them up and stuffing them in the bin. And there are those who have seen so many of these letters now that they can't bring themselves to open them at all, and destroy them unread.

And this is understandable.

I did the same thing while at Barings. A statement would be on my desk each morning relating to the illegal trading account. In the first few months I would look through it and try to work out strategies to possibly recoup the losses. As the losses increased, often dramatically, I'd slide the statement off the desk, into the drawer at my feet without the slightest peak. As I slipped even further into the mire, I told the staff that I no longer needed the statement and it should be filed away immediately after it was printed.

But denial never works, and it is definitely not a solution.

Typically, what these letters might say is that your lenders will be looking to retrieve as much of their money as quickly as possible. This isn't the best situation for you, but it does mean that a complete review of your financial situation is required. And this is actually a good thing. If you think there are problems there, the likelihood is that you are right, and the sooner you can begin to address them, the better things will be.

Anger

The stage that follows denial is often that of anger. There has to be someone to blame and in most cases you can find at least one. In different times any number of public figures might find themselves in the stocks, but times have changed. Bad advice was common currency in the recent years, but the reality is that we should all have probably been asking more questions than we were, and most of us need to shoulder some blame for our own situations.

Becoming accountable for any difficult period in your life is a hard step, but I like to think that it is the first step in the right direction.

From experience, I can say that the anger is a totally wasted emotion. The energy that you are using up in a rage can be better channelled in the direction of finding a solution to your money worries. Of course, it's hard not to get angry, especially for those of you who have worked all their life to achieve something, and it is meaninglessly frittered away by events beyond your control. But the truth is that the anger itself will get you nothing, and bring you nowhere.

I am not the first to grasp this concept. Typically I am, and always have been, very placid in nature but this was severely tested when I was transferred from Hoechst Prison to Tanah Merah in Singapore to serve my four-and-a-half-year sentence. The cells were small, six metres by nine metres, and three of us were expected to share that space. It was cramped and very, very hot. At daybreak, the mercury would have leapt past the 100°F mark and stayed there all day. Unexpectedly, it got even hotter in the cell at night, as the sun had been baking the concrete floors outside all day and the heat would keep rising, forcing itself in on top of us. It was impossible to regulate the heat in your body, it was impossible to keep clean, and the one thing that you used to look forward to most was a shower.

The opportunity for this always came at 7 a.m. The guards would walk behind the cells and turn on the water. You could see them through the wire mesh on the back of the cells as they meandered their way along the prison block. The prison was overcrowded and 'E' Block, my home for four years, was the furthest from the water source. More than half of the time, we would still not have been released from our cells by 8 a.m., when the same guard would walk the same route and turn the water off. I started off pleading for the taps to be left open a little while longer, to no avail. Soon after, I resorted to shouting and hollering abuse. I was getting more and more angry and incredibly wound up. If there had been anything to throw or break I would have done both, but there was nothing. At 8.15 a.m., the cell doors would open and the only thing on my mind was physical confrontation. My target was the guard who turned the water on and off, and I would make a beeline straight for him, shouting abuse as I moved. My insurrection would always be swiftly and quickly put down by a number of his fellow guards and I invariably felt worse than before.

Slowly, I realised that I was wasting my time. The only person getting angry was myself and the only person I was damaging was myself. I came to realise that there are certain things in your life that you can influence and certain things you cannot. The important thing is that you do not let the things that you can't influence worry you, and instead focus on the things that you can do something about. The guard was going to carry out his duties regardless of my protestations. Anger is only useful if it is channelled correctly. Getting angry about a debt situation that has already occurred is wasteful, as there's nothing in this that anger can change. What you should be focusing on is finding a solution and anger will generally only make that more difficult.

If we apply these same principals to financial problems, it is apparent that there is no point dwelling too much on any personal failures when so many of the causes were beyond your control. It should be an education though, and it is important that we all learn it so we can help prevent this from ever happening again, either to us as individuals, or to us as a country.

Depression

As we progress through denial and anger, the next stage is potentially the most damaging and it something to watch out for as keenly as possible. Once depression starts, it can be difficult to control, particularly if you try and cope with it on your own.

Being in financial difficulty is the last thing that anyone might have expected and it can overwhelm and frustrate in equal measure, and, while it will affect everyone differently, it can certainly cause an immense amount of sadness. Some people may have lost their job, or their car or, in extreme cases, their home might be at risk. All of these things can be damaging, particularly to our pride.

When I was on remand in Germany prior to returning to Singapore, there were many things to occupy my mind. I was mounting a defence against the charges in Singapore at the same time as writing a book to sell in order to pay my legal fees. Strangely enough, I didn't have too much time to spare. In Singapore, the situation was very different, there was nothing to occupy me, so naturally I started to think over things that happened in the past. Part of that process is to think about the things that you could have done differently. In retrospect, this is a kind of wishful thinking and I personally regard it as one of the most debilitating things that anybody can do. What has happened has happened, and the past is the past. The most important thing is that you focus on the future and find ways to move forward with your life. Depression for me exists on a downward spiral that gathers momentum the more negatively you think. The key for me is to slow that spiral down. I've been driven to the edge many times, simply by things that I am thinking. In prison I witnessed many inmates struggling to come to terms with their thoughts, and looking for the sharpest corner of the wall to create the maximum damage to themselves with the minimum fuss. Financial stress has clearly been behind a number of tragic events of late, when people have been unable to see any way out other than to take their own lives. The rise in the suicide rate in Ireland is a concern for us all, and while this is far too complicated a subject to address here in a meaningful way, there are many support systems available, and people who have been in similar situations who want to help. These will be listed at the end of this book, and these services can give all of us options, awareness and choices that we may not have realised were there before.

The question I get asked most often is 'What would you have done differently if you had your time again?' The genuine answer is that I would do almost all of it differently. Of course, I do not know whether that is entirely true but I do know that I am never going to be afforded that opportunity again in this lifetime, so thinking about it is a waste of time. The same thinking applies to debt. Don't tear yourself up, you need all that strength to move forward.

Perspective can be a funny thing, and one benefit that so much change can bring is that it can allow you to realise what is really important to you. For me, I was driven by a need for success and a huge fear of failure, two forces which walked hand in hand. I had an exalted opinion of what the kind of success I strove for looked like, making big decisions, being at the top of the tree. Now I realise that just as much success can come from putting food on the table for your children. And what this tells me is that I prefer the post-crash version of myself to the one that went before.

Acceptance

Ideally the start of this cycle quickly takes over from anger and resentment, and, as difficult as acceptance of your situation is, it signifies that someone is coming to terms with their difficulties and dealing with them in a meaningful way. They might still be in debt – things don't get better overnight – but they are able to accept that they might not earn quite as much, or have the trappings of life that previously looked so good, particularly on paper. They certainly aren't alone in these struggles and that is important to realise. But most importantly, they can start to engage and communicate their problems, to find the path through them, and there is always a path. An exit from debt can take a little time, likely a minimum of twelve months, but a solution will be far more clearly visible than at any time in the past. And to get there, each and every solution requires a plan.

I had no such plan when I was released from prison; I really did not know what the future would hold and sometimes my behaviour patterns started to slip back into those that were destructive rather than constructive. I existed in three-month phases and could not see a longer horizon. I was truly remorseful for everything that happened at Barings and all of the people that it affected, but eventually I had to move on.

It can often be the case that personal debt affects those around us as we struggle to cope; it may have caused some pain and resentment but moving towards a positive stage of acceptance will be welcomed and eventually applauded by all of the people around you. This is the way out, and what everyone has been waiting for.

New Start

Life will move on and slowly, with a plan in place, we can take back control of our financial affairs. The phone will ring and you won't ignore it, the doorbell will chime and you won't panic to see who is there. Whilst we still may not *welcome* a letter from the bank, it won't be the harbinger of doom that it was. It is a time where it's possible to make meaningful and hopefully long-standing changes to your life, based on hard lessons, but which will turn out to be a positive thing. And we will ask more questions, challenge what we are told, but most of all we will understand more about finance than we ever did before.

Debt is going to be among us for a while, but it should not be unspoken and it should not be feared. And, please remember, it is absolutely possible to become debt free again.

3

The New Insolvency Legislation

Nobody has ever accused the process of change of being too efficient, or complained that it happens too quickly. It is often, by its very nature, something necessarily reactive rather than proactive. The new insolvency legislation in Ireland is no different in this respect.

The economic shift in Ireland from boom to gloom was, of course, seismic in its proportions, and addressing it was never going to be a simple task. For many people, fear and financial uncertainty have become the norm, and plotting a path back to stability is a very real challenge.

As a nation, however, this situation has presented us with a major opportunity: to review and ultimately change the debt laws in Ireland. In my own opinion, this opportunity was partially taken but in a number of areas the new legislation has over-promised and under-delivered.

To give the background, in 2003, the Free Legal Advice Centres published a report on the treatment of credit and debt in Ireland. A follow-up report came in 2009, which presented the very clear conclusion that a more modern approach to debt was required. The existing legislation was draconian in its approach to dealing with the problem and did little more than exacerbate the fears that those in difficulty were facing. Many lobby groups entered the debate and pressed for an alteration to the way that people who can't afford to pay their debts are treated by the system. As the economic decline gathered pace, so did the problems facing people with debt. The debt pile, both individual and national, had grown far beyond anyone's worst case scenarios and the calls for reform grew louder. In 2010, the Law Reform Commission (LRC) conducted a review of the legal treatment of debt and published their findings. The LRC recommended a fundamental shift away from the courts in dealing with debt and the modernisation of the laws that currently existed. In total, the report made about 200 recommendations for reform and included a draft personal insolvency bill.

From that point, it took another two years for the personal insolvency legislation to be published. The main impetus for this did not always come from the government, as you might think, but was actually part of the terms of the bailout deal that had been agreed with Ireland by 'The Troika' (the collective term for the EU, IMF and the ECB) who argued that Ireland must change the way that they dealt with this issue. Unsurprisingly, the Troika still remain the driving force behind many changes that we see in how banks are currently dealing with indebted customers. Eventually, in 2012, the government published the long-awaited personal insolvency legislation. The bill was signed into law at the end of the same year. Whilst it does represent significant change, in time, my concern is that it will go down as a huge missed opportunity.

Many years ago I had my own experience of personal debt. Admittedly I had already lost hundreds of millions of pounds by my own hand. I had made financial reparations to the police in Singapore and issued personal apologies to the nation of Singapore, but I had never really been saddled with any overbearing personal debt. That all changed on 4 July 1999.

I'd been looking forward to this day for some time, but the date was an equal mix of excitement and trepidation. Since the day that my sentence had been handed down in the Singapore High Court, I knew that my date of release was 3 July 1999. Normally you are released by 8 a.m. but, because of the high-profile nature of my case, I wasn't going to be allowed to walk freely around the wide streets of Singapore. I was effectively being deported and banned from ever returning.

So my release day was going to be very different from most. I'd kept a diary for much of the last four years in simple copybooks that you were allowed to buy with your prison work earnings. Very early on in the morning, I was released from my cell and delivered up to a room in a more general area. My companion for the day was a paper shredder and the mountain of journals that I had kept throughout that period. I had to remove the staples by hand and slowly place each and every page through the shredding machine. Four years in prison in Singapore was obliterated in a little under two hours of destruction.

Later that evening, thirteen or fourteen hours after the traditional release time, I was delivered to Changi Airport and placed in a holding cell until the British Airways flight was ready to leave, shortly before midnight. I was the last one onto the plane and as I arrived at my seat, my lawyer was already present. The usual pleasantries were exchanged, food eaten and night slipped into day as 3 July became 4 July. It was straight down to business however. A speech had been written for my arrival at Heathrow Airport and the waiting media. The curve ball that I had never seen coming was an injunction that the liquidators wanted to serve upon me as we hit the tarmac in London. The injunction was against any existing assets, cash and also against any earnings from that point forward. The only negotiable point was the size of the injunction. There wasn't much negotiation, to be honest. I was pretty much willing to sign any sum away, as I knew I hadn't stolen any money and that there was no hidden treasure. The liquidators, through my lawyer, had full visibility of what I had and what I was likely to earn over the next few months. I suggested a couple of billion, preferring to be as ludicrous as possible. As outlandish as the figure then sounded, it now pales into insignificance when you think of the recklessness of Celtic Tiger Ireland. The figure that was settled on was £100 million – mere pocket change!

On landing, I was rushed straight to a hotel room in the Hilton. So far so good, but after four-and-a-half years in prison, I had imagined the waiting guests might be prettier than three, rather rotund, liquidators. We quickly signed the injunction and from that point on I would have a £100 million noose around my neck.

This in many ways coloured my view of debt from that point forward. I had no money left, but while I still retained an opportunity to earn, the liquidators would have a lien over any monies that I was paid from that point forward. After a certain point, however, the size really made no difference, because if you can't pay, you simply can't pay. Debt, as I will refer to many times, is an affordability issue. Once you've crossed that point, the size of the debt becomes irrelevant.

So what do the new debt rules actually mean for people who are in financial difficulty? There are a number of different measures, all which will be explained in more detail later. There's the introduction of automatic discharge from bankruptcy after three years as opposed to the previous twelve. There are new structured arrangements for people in debt that will allow for some debt write-down, and the creation of a new body, the Insolvency Service of Ireland (ISI) to supervise and control the industry. The new system also introduces three non-judicial debt resolution processes, a Debt Relief Notice (DRN), a Debt Settlement Arrangement (DSA) and a Personal Insolvency Arrangement (PIA). Each resolution comes with its own rules, terms and conditions.

Lorcan O'Connor will head the new ISI. He has vast experience in this area and he will be aided by a staff that is expected to grow quite rapidly. It will need to as, in my opinion, we are still only scratching the surface of the problem. The ISI will be a statutory body responsible for all matters in this area. They will be tasked with developing guidelines for insolvency procedures, providing the necessary information to both the public and practitioners, as well as maintaining the appropriate statistics in regard to insolvency and regulating insolvency practitioners.

Undoubtedly the most controversial part of their role will be guiding and overseeing the restrictions that are going to be imposed on those people who are seeking a debt deal. Any form of debt resolution comes with an element of pain. From the point of acceptance through to the point of resolution, a certain amount of sacrifice is unavoidable. In the majority of cases, the hope is that these will simply represent life-style changes, but there will be influence exerted over how those who benefit from a debt deal are allowed to spend money. The responsibility for publishing the guidelines on what represents a reasonable standard of living and reasonable living expenses lies with the ISI and the Department for Justice & Equality. In determining what constitutes reasonable living expenses for a family or individual, certain key factors will be considered: the need for a car, childcare costs, housing costs and special circumstances such as health conditions.

It's in this area that worries and fears of those involved can spiral out of control. Much of the media reporting on this part of the legislation has been sensational to date and directed at the onerous nature of the methods used to arrive at a reasonable standard of living. A brief look at the fifteen measures that they are looking to base their affordability decisions on makes that very clear.

Expenditure category	A guide to what is included in each expenditure category.	For a single adult of working age living alone this comes to a monthly total of:	For a single adult of working age living alone this comes to an annual total of:
Food	The expenditure on food is based on a balanced, nutritious diet. The consensual budget standards model is premised on a healthy lifestyle.	€247.04	€2,964.48
Clothing	Clothing and footwear for all seasons, including accessories.	€35.73	€428.76
Personal Care	Personal hygiene and grooming items.	€33.40	€400.80
Health	Medications, and visits to a General Practitioner, Optician, Dentist, etc. It also includes small items such as plasters, antiseptic, and over-the-counter medicines.	€31.09	€373.08

Household Goods	Furniture, appliances, cleaning products, etc. Single adults of working age living in an urban area are assumed to be living in a rented furnished studio apartment.	€31.47	€377.64
Household Services	Vital household related services such as waste charges, getting an annual boiler service, and having chimneys swept.	€28.61	€343.32
Communications	Telephone, postage and basic internet; an internet dongle/wireless connection at €4.69 per week and phone credit at €5.00 per week.	€43.45	€521.40
Education	The minimum education needs of a household as decided by the focus groups. This category includes uniforms, books, and stationery where applicable and also adult education.	€24.50	€294.00
Transport	The cost of a car is allowed where public transport is inadequate to get to work, school and the local shop.	€136.29 for public transport costs or €240.13 if a car is necessary	€1,635.48 for public transport costs or €2,881.56 if a car is necessary
Household Energy	Electricity and home heating fuel. Electricity and heating costs come from the CSO Household Budget Survey.	€48.87 electricity €57.31 heating	€586.44 electricity €687.72 heating

Insurance	Home insurance and also car insurance where a car is needed. Note that the ISI model does not ordinarily include private health insurance though this may be included in some circumstances where warranted.	€12.22 home contents €25.91 car insurance where applicable	€146.64 home contents €310.92 car insurance where applicable
Savings and Contingencies	Savings and life assurance (for households with dependents). For a single person, savings at €5 a week are assumed as is €5 a week to be put aside for contingencies and emergencies.	€43.33	€519.96
Social Inclusion and Participation	At €28.97 a week, the minimum considered necessary for participation and inclusion. It includes sports activities and social events such as visits to the cinema. The ISI model does not factor in the cost of a holiday.	€125.97	€1,511.64
Housing	Rent of mortgage payments may clearly be catered for		
Childcare	This area will be given careful consideration, and is still being debated.		

A summary of the measures introduced by the ISI would suggest 'for the purposes of the Act, a reasonable standard of living is one which meets a person's physical, psychological and social needs'. Under the ISI model, a 'reasonable standard of living' does not mean that a person should live at a level of luxury but neither does it mean that a person should only live at subsistence level. A debtor should, of course, be able to participate in the life of the community, as other citizens do. It should be possible for the debtor 'to eat nutritious food … to have clothes for different weather and situations, to keep the home clean and tidy, to have furniture and equipment at home for rest and recreation, to be able to devote some time to leisure activities, and to read books, newspapers and watch television'.

The following is a quotation from the text of the ISI's published guidelines on this topic:

As a general principle, the ISI wishes to see debtors retaining the autonomy to make their own choices as to what is best for them, though necessarily within the constraints of reasonableness and the overall expenditure limits. Thus, while the focus groups have decided that cable or satellite television subscriptions are not necessary and that allowance for a SAORVIEW approved set-top-box or television is sufficient, a debtor may choose to retain such a subscription by prioritising it within his or her budget. So long as an applicant for one of the three new personal insolvency processes

under the Act comes within the overall headline figure
for reasonable living expenses, the ISI will not be pre-
scriptive in terms of what the applicant can or cannot
spend their money on.

Only where an applicant spends in excess of what is
considered to be reasonable under these guidelines will
it become necessary for the AI or PIP to look at his or
her spending across the categories of expenditure.

*(By permission of the ISI, 'Guidelines on a reason-
able standard of living and reasonable living expenses',
p. 27)*

To my mind, there is a danger here of moving
in the wrong direction by being too restrictive. I am reminded of one of the first books
that I had to study at school, *Little Dorrit* by
Charles Dickens. This book was first published
in the mid-nineteenth century and is a satire
of the failings of government and society of
the period. You can imagine why there might
be a resonance in the present day. The focus of
much of the anger in this book was directed at
the debtors prisons, which were, at the time,
the way in which society dealt with those who
could not pay their debts. There they had to
work, often in irons, and were charged a daily
rate for their keep, on top of that which they

originally owed. The prison in the story was Marshalsea, where Dicken's own father had been imprisoned for his debts, and where Little Amy Dorrit's family now resided. Whilst she was free to go during the day, they would all return at night. All the guilt and humiliation caused by bad debt are included in what could be described as a Victorian credit crunch story. If *Little Dorrit* was published a year ago you would have been forgiven for thinking that it was not wholly a work of fiction. In the light of what has happened in Wall Street, Iceland and, most relevantly, the banks in this country, the trail of sadness caused by bad debt seems particularly raw. I am concerned that if there is a lack of flexibility in the current guidelines, Ireland will become the modern-day equivalent of Marshalsea, and it is not beyond the bounds of possibility that, like Amy Dorrit, our children could be burdened with the debt of their parents.

It is for that reason that the new insolvency legislation represents a missed opportunity. Something meaningful was required but, to my mind, some measures have stopped way too short, others have gone too far. The new legislation retains a punitive aspect, and whilst I think that everyone can see that there is a need for a certain amount of pain, the purpose must be to carve a path upon which people can move forward. On this point, it seems to fail. For instance, it is not wholly clear why there is an upper limit of €3 million on those who can avail of the PIA. It seems an arbitrary figure, based solely on the idea that those who borrowed more need to be punished for longer, and effectively pushed towards bankruptcy. This is wrong and goes against the practice of most successful insolvency legislature that exists outside the jurisdiction. In many ways it cements the idea that the overriding purpose of this legislation was to remain largely punitive. There is no doubt that tens of thousands of people were waiting for its implementation, but the sad fact is that thousands have also been left disappointed.

We live in unprecedented times, and the measures to combat the problems need to be more far-reaching than those that are set before us. The missed opportunity is that there is a system in the UK that has worked well for decades. The solution, many feel, should have been to copy this legislation and the measures available in the UK to deal with debt. There are three formal solutions available there: Debt Management Plans, Individual Voluntary Arrangements (IVA) or Company Voluntary Arrangements (CVA), and Bankruptcy. Each provide a solution to your personal problem, are efficient in dealing with your creditors and conclude your debt solution in a more timely manner. The IVA and CVA arrangements have no upper limit and work well. There is no doubt that there is an element of abuse in the system but that is for the regulators to control, together with the police. The debt solutions in Ireland are more conditional, thereby making them more restrictive and, ultimately, harsher than their UK equivalent.

I believe that the policymakers lost sight of the fact that we are dealing with wholesale indebtedness, not brought about by individual malfeasance but a wider disaster that swept away everything in its path. Exceptional circumstances require exceptional measures and I think we have been presented with a long-term solution to what is essentially a short-term problem.

The part of the legislation that might have some meaningful attempt at resolution of the debt problem will be the PIA. This could result in the level of personal debt falling to more acceptable levels if used correctly. Ultimately it will rely on the Central Bank to ensure that banks fully engage in the process and do not exercise the veto that they will hold in accepting the arrangement. It might not always be their preferred option and they may continue to try and put the borrower through the mangle for a time, to get the best result for the bank.

Personally though, I do try to look at these things as though the glass was half full, and try to find some positive in adversity. It's admittedly difficult in this case, but there are opportunities here that I think should not be missed. Firstly as individuals, regardless of whether this is the best of all possible solutions, it is a good thing that ultimately we are learning to take tighter control of our finances, ask more questions, not place blind faith in advisers, or even sometimes legislators; empowering yourself with knowledge allows us to ask better and more valuable questions, both of others and of ourselves. And as individuals, if we can get through that stage, we will be better placed to create a safer and more stable future.

4

Debt Relief Notices

The new personal insolvency regime has been designed to offer a lifeline to those that are struggling to contain and manage their liabilities. The legislation has ensured, through instigating strict rules and procedures, that the path to freedom from debt will not be an easy route but it is a step in the right direction. Three different solutions are being made available to three different types of borrower: those with pretty much no residual income after taking into account reasonable living expenses; those who have no property assets but have more than €60 per month of residual income; and those that have property and debts not exceeding €3 million.

Each of the new procedures are non-judicial debt resolution processes. Perhaps the most positive development that will result from going through this process will be an element of certainty. Families struggling to keep their heads above water could be afforded a far more secure situation whereby they know how much income they have each month, where it will be apportioned and, most importantly, there will be a light at the end of the tunnel, when the arrangement put in place will come to an end. Typically borrowers might be looking at no longer than a five-year period but it will enable people to draw a line under their troubles and move on.

Life will almost certainly start again with the new regime. The worrying calls and letters will stop and rather than hiding away, just as my mother used to hide from the 'Telly Man', it will be possible to get back to normal and, when the knock on the door comes, it will be only one of the kids' friends. Striking a debt deal will mean that families will have to stick to a strict budget, but, in return, they will have a chance at a new financial future.

Goldman Sachs described the period from 2008 on as a lost decade and, to my mind, they have been exactly right. Many people will be five years into the hardest financial times that they have ever faced and, if they have to use one of the new arrangements to resolve debt issues, it will last another five. But then it will be over. The new legislation is a step forwards, and, most importantly, will be on the statute books for years to come. Ideally it will also be reviewed as soon as the nation is back on its feet and a large number of these arrangements have run their course. Perhaps there will be further improvement.

The vast majority of people in financial stress want to do the right thing. They feel morally obliged to pay everybody but, without assistance, this often only works for a while. Eventually they might start paying everybody a little less, using one credit card to pay another and then ultimately look to skip payments. This month it may be the credit card, next month the car insurance. As long as you make a payment to the one or the other this month, it's possible to believe that you are doing ok and keeping everybody happy. If you are a homeowner, your mortgage should always receive priority; not only does it make sense, it is expected and this new legislation does little to alter that fact. But the new legislation does provide a plan to facilitate managing other, unsecured debt, and this is the DRN.

A DRN is the first new measure made available under the new Insolvency Act. It allows for the write-off of qualifying unsecured debt of up to €20,000, subject to a three-year supervision period. This type of relief is ideal for a person with no income and no assets, subject to certain limits, who has no realistic prospect of being able to pay their debts within the next three years. The published guidelines of the ISI state that, 'The Insolvency Act provides that to be eligible for a DRN the debtor must have net disposable income, calculated in accordance with *subsection (5)*, of €60 or less a month.' The Act, details of which are fully available to the public through the ISI and other sources listed at the end of this book, sets out the ways in which this disposable income is calculated.

In simple terms, the elements which constitute the income and expenditure are as follows:

Income

- Salary or wages
- Welfare benefits (other than child benefit)
- Pension income
- Contributions from other household members
- Any other income

While pension income will be calculated as part of this process, it appears that anyone availing of the DRN will not be obliged to draw down the whole of any 'pension pot' early as part of this agreement.

Social Welfare payments will be treated as income, except for Child Benefit which will remain outside this process.

'Windfall amounts' and gifts are also covered in this process, when they are above €500. If the debtor does receive an amount in excess of this figure, half of this will have to be surrendered and will be distributed to creditors.

Expenditure

- · Reasonable living expenses
- · Income tax payable
- · Social insurance contributions
- · Payments of excluded debts
- · Payments of excludable debts that are not permitted debts
- · Such other levies and charges on the debtor's income as may be prescribed

The listing here refers to 'excluded debts', in other words debts that are secured, like a mortgage or a car loan. Secured debts will not be part of the debt settlement under a DRN arrangement, so payments of these would still have to be made. The types of debt that are typically covered by the DRN, and which will then be written off at the end of the process, will be debts such as credit card debt, overdraft or arrears in utility bills.

Excludable and permitted debts are also mentioned, and these are worth explaining in more detail also. 'Excluded debts' are debts which cannot be part of this relief process, and these are debts that refer to orders made through the Family Law Courts, such as orders for payments to a spouse or to children. Fines imposed by the courts do not qualify, or orders made by the court for payments under the Proceeds of Crime Act.

'Permitted debts' are debts which are not automatically included, but which can be included with the consent of the creditor. These include tax payments, the Household Charge, or, an area which can affect many people living in apartments, arrears in management fees and annual service charges. These are what are referred to as 'excludable debts' which then become 'permitted debts' should the creditor consent.

Of course, the elephant in the room in this scenario is what exactly constitutes 'reasonable living expenses'. What is important to one person, say for example having a car, or a subscription to a gym, might not be the same for someone else who lives near good public transport and enjoys the cinema. It's not an exact science, but the Act recognises this, and a degree of flexibility has been built into this process to cater for specific needs. Again, guidelines to this are available on the ISI website, and these will be updated annually.

After income and expenditure is taken into account, what remains is the creditor's 'net disposable income' which, in order to qualify for the DRN, must be less than €60 a month.

The process for application is very simple, and should be made to the ISI via an Approved Intermediary (AI) such as the Money Advice and Budgeting Service (MABS). When making your application, the AI will help you complete a Prescribed Financial Statement (PFS), giving full details of your financial situation. Obviously, this must be filled in with complete honesty and transparency. The applicant will also be subject to an asset test as an applicant for a DRN cannot have assets worth more than €400. They will tend to be renting their home, rather than being a homeowner. There are some exemptions from the asset test, however. These are €6,000 for household goods, any materials or equipment needed for educational purposes up to the end of second-level education, one item of personal jewellery up to a value of €750 and a motor vehicle with a value not exceeding €2,000.

There are also some important conditions that you must consider. During the three-year supervision period, you may not get credit of €650 or more from any source, either on your own or as part of a joint application with someone else, without informing that source that you have a DRN. Equally so, you must tell the ISI of any change in your personal circumstances, such as an increase in income. If your financial position improves during the supervision period, you may have to repay part of your debts.

One final aspect of the DRN worth noting is that it will also be possible in certain circumstances to 'buy' your way out of the DRN. Once you have been approved and been accepted into this process, if your personal circumstances improve enough for you to pay 50% of the amount owed as part of the DRN, the process will end.

The most significant development of entering a DRN for most people, however, will be that creditors will not be able to pursue any action against you for recovery of debts covered by the process. This will last the entire length of the supervision period, which is typically three years. Imagine the relief. You still may not have much money but the horizon of how long you have to deal with your debt problems will have shrunk considerably. Not only will you have more disposable income at the end of the process, not only will the phone calls and letters stop but at the end of the process you will be largely debt free.

Example 1 – Sarah – DRN

Sarah is in her late 20s and lives at home with her parents and has no dependent children. She was recently made redundant from her job as a secretary when her employer was forced into liquidation. She is now unemployed and her only income is the €188 per week (€815 per month) that she receives as social welfare.

She owns a car valued at €1,500 but owns no other assets other than her simple household effects. She has savings of €3,000 at the credit union but has €12,500 in borrowings and a further €3,000 outstanding on her credit card. Her monthly repayments on these loans total €200 and she is unable to pay this given her current financial predicament. After paying for her weekly essentials such as food, clothes, rent and so on, she is left with €20 per month.

The first step is for Sarah to meet with an AI such as MABS to discuss her options. The AI will review Sarah's situation and will assess whether she meets the qualifying criteria, as set out in the legislation as follows:

- Has Sarah less than €60 per month available after reasonable living expenses?
- Are Sarah's total loans less than the €20,000 threshold?
- Are Sarah's assets below the €2,000 value for a qualifying motor vehicle and €6,000 for other assets?

Sarah will qualify for the DRN on the basis that she meets all of these criteria.

Subject to Sarah signing a declaration that the facts outlined are correct, she can apply for a DRN from a recognised intermediary who will send all the required documents to the ISI for approval. The ISI will then facilitate the application for a DRN for Sarah. A three-year moratorium then applies, during which none of Sarah's creditors can pursue her for repayment of her debts. At the end of the three-year period, her debts will be written off and Sarah will be debt free.

Example 2 – Steve – DRN

Steve is a 23-year-old single male, living alone in a city centre flat which he rents privately at a cost of €600 a month. He doesn't have or need a car. He is in full-time employment and his take home pay is €1,550 a month. He has credit card debt of €11,000 and owes a credit union another €6,000. He is finding it impossible to make the monthly payments on top of his rent and all his other bills and wonders if he can get a DRN. Steve should check the eligibility criteria on the ISI website before visiting an AI. He can also get a list of AIs from the ISI website. Amongst other matters, the AI will check whether Steve meets the eligibility criteria of having €60 or less disposable income each month.

The AI will use Table 1 (one adult household, no vehicle) which shows the monthly set costs to be €900.08. To this is added his rent of €600 a month, having been assessed as reasonable by the AI in accordance with the criteria on assessing housing costs set out by the ISI, making his reasonable living expenses €1,500.08.

The AI will make the following calculation:

Monthly income after income tax and social insurance contributions	€1,550.00
Total set costs	€900.08
Rent / mortgage	€600.00
Childcare	None
Special circumstances	None
Reasonable living expenses	€1,500.08
Net disposable income	€49.92

Steve will be eligible for a DRN.

Example 3 – Don and Aoife – DRN

In this example the guidelines are applied in the case of a couple where only one of them is in receipt of income and bears all of the reasonable living expenses of the household.

Don and Aoife are a married couple in their 20s, living in accommodation provided by their local authority for which they pay €65 a month. Neither is employed at the moment but Don is seeking work and receiving jobseeker's allowance. They do not have a car. They have two children, aged 3 and 8. Don is in arrears on a personal loan he took out with a bank two years ago when he was working. The outstanding balance is just over €12,000. He cannot see where he can get the money to pay off his creditors and thinks that a DRN might be an answer.

Don should look at the eligibility criteria on the ISI website before visiting an AI. Amongst other matters, the AI will check whether Don meets the eligibility criteria of having €60 or less net disposable income each month. Don receives €188 in jobseeker's allowance, plus a payment of €124.80 in respect of Aoife who is a Qualified Adult. In addition, he receives a total of €59.60 a week in Qualified Child Increase payments. Child benefit payments are not included. His total reckonable income comes to €372.40 a week or €1,619.32 a month.

Using the relevant reasonable costs table (Two-Parent Household, one or more children, no vehicle) the AI will take set costs of €1,305.77 for the two adults and add €223.22 for the two children (€46.09 for a pre-school child and €177.13 for a child of primary school age). To this is added €65 for their housing costs, having been assessed as reasonable by the AI in accordance with the criteria on assessing housing costs, giving reasonable living expenses of €1,593.99 a month for the household.

The AI will make the following calculation:

Monthly income after income tax and social insurance contributions	€1,619.32
Total set costs	€1,528.99
Rent / mortgage	€65.00
Childcare	None
Special circumstances	None
Reasonable living expenses	€1,593.99
Net disposable income	€25.33

Don and Aoife are eligible for a DRN.

(Worked examples provided courtesy of the ISI)

5

Debt Settlement Arrangements

The second process, the Debt Settlement Arrangement (DSA) allows for the agreed settlement of unsecured debt, with no limit involved, normally over a period of five years. As with the DRN, 'unsecured debts' are the focus of this arrangement, which covers debts such as credit cards, overdrafts or utilities, and not a mortgage or car loan where there is collateral over the loan.

It is most suited to those people who have some capacity to make some level of repayments to their creditors but fall outside the scope of the DRN, possibly because their net income after expenses is too high.

Unlike the DRN, however, you will need the services of a Personal Insolvency Practitioner (PIP) to guide you through the process. A PIP is a qualified financial expert who has been approved by the ISI. PIPs do charge a fee for the work they do, which will be built into the arrangement, but their fees are entirely regulated by the ISI, and they are essentially working to help the debtor manage their situation.

The first step is that the PIP will guide you through the process of completing a PFS. This will be a full and honest disclosure of all the details of your finances, which will then be used as part of your application for a DSA. This is essential for your own state of mind and will allow you to formulate a plan with the PIP that is both sustainable and achievable. This, as mentioned previously, is a powerful exercise in itself in understanding exactly where you stand financially.

The next step the PIP will guide you through is the obtaining of a Protective Certificate. This is a certificate which protects you from enforcement proceedings during the period where a sustainable arrangement is being proposed and negotiated on your behalf. The PIP will apply for this on your behalf through the ISI, who will verify that all the details are correct. They will then pass it onto the courts who, when satisfied with the application, will issue a Protective Certificate.

Following this, the work starts in earnest, and the PIP will prepare a proposal for your creditors. In order for a proposal to be successful, it must be accepted by 65% of all the creditors involved. Once the proposal has been formally accepted, the day-to-day responsibility for its administration lies with your PIP and you will not have to deal with any of the creditors involved again for the duration of the process.

The most important piece of information is that, as you will only be allowed to enter a DSA once, it is vital that it is realistic and most importantly sustainable. You have the opportunity to correct a debt problem at this point, but once and only once through this channel, so, if this is the best route to take, it's vital to make the most of it.

Exact details of the terms of this scheme can be obtained through the ISI, but one of the points to note is that no more than 25% of the debts which would be covered by this arrangement can have been built up in the 6 months prior to making an application. The reason for this is that this arrangement will result in a percentage of the creditor's debt being written off, so there understandably needs to be some safeguards to ensure debts were not amassed with the intention of entering the scheme.

Once the arrangement is in place, each debtor engaging in this process will agree a budget during the course of the arrangement and, as with the DRN, there will be an assessment of what would constitute reasonable living expenses as part of this process.

Ultimately, the decision on the reasonableness or otherwise of living expenses in this instance will be a matter for the creditors to determine on a case-by-case basis in accordance with the terms and guidelines of the Act. This is subject to the provision that the debtor will not be required to make payments of an amount so high that he or she would not have sufficient income to maintain a reasonable standard of living. If a PIP has put forward a proposal which contains unrealistic or disproportionate living expenses, there is a strong likelihood that the creditors would vote against acceptance of the arrangement on that basis. The reasons for this are again understandable, as every creditor, including the banks, are ideally looking to recover all of their money, and this is their starting point. However, they also have to be rational in securing the best deal that they can possibly get. On this basis, it would not really make sense to deliver the debtor to the door of abject poverty, disincentivising them from continuing with the process, and leading it to fail within a short period of time. If that were to happen, the distressed borrower will likely be left holding only one card, the bankruptcy option, and this will more than likely see the creditors recovering next to nothing.

The starting position of the creditors and the debtor will be at different ends of the spectrum and they will ideally end up somewhere approaching the middle. Common sense and reasonableness will be the most important parts of the process, and I see the PIP's key role as delivering both parties to this point as smoothly and painlessly as possible within the guidelines of the legislation.

Hand in hand with this aspect of the negotiation process is that it is important that individuals in financial difficulty, who are also in employment, be given some incentive to continue working. A reduction to the income level which that individual would have if they were to be unemployed and in receipt of social welfare would obviously be detrimental to this. In the context of working debtors entering into DSAs, the individuals involved should be able to retain some of the money they are earning before the balance of their income goes to discharge the debt. There will be a need for PIPs to engage with creditors and debtors in order to ensure that workable arrangements are put in place in this instance. Creditors have a real interest in the debtor being at work, and getting a real financial benefit from working, as this will potentially allow them to pay off a greater amount of their debts over a period of time. The arrangement is clearly in everyone's best interests. A balance will then have to be struck between the allocation of earnings to creditors and their retention by the debtor, and this will vary from individual to individual. Again, these negotiations will happen with you and your PIP, and then between the PIP and your creditors.

Banks may try to continue to operate outside of the process, believing that direct contact/negotiation with the borrower will achieve better results for themselves but the distressed borrower will be able to avail of the protection afforded by these formal arrangements. Realigning these kind of divergent aims will ideally be both the role and the skill of the PIP.

Example 1 – Emma – DSA

This example will show how the application of these guidelines may demonstrate that a debtor is ineligible to apply for a DRN and that, in such circumstances, a DSA may remain a possibility for the insolvent debtor.

Emma is self-employed on a part-time basis as a physiotherapist and earns €2,600 after tax a month. She is a single mother with a son aged five who needs paid childcare on the days Emma works. Emma privately rents her home and pays €300 a month in rent. She needs a car to transport her son to school and to get to her job. She has a 2003 Peugeot 106 worth €1,900 which she owns outright. Fees for part-time childcare come to €500 a month. Emma has a personal loan from her bank with an outstanding balance of €15,200. She is finding it difficult to make the repayments and seeks advice.

Emma should look at the eligibility criteria for DRNs and DSAs on the ISI website before proceeding. From the information on the website she can calculate her reasonable living expenses and work out her net disposable income. As this does not meet the eligibility criteria for a DRN, Emma will need to contact a PIP rather than an AI. Emma should obtain the details of registered PIPs from the ISI website and contact one of them.

The PIP will use the appropriate table of reasonable living expenses (one adult household, one or more children, vehicle), which shows the monthly set costs to be €1,271.63. This is made up of €1,066.75 for the adult and €204.88 for the child. To this is added

€500 a month for the cost of part-time child-care and the €300 a month Emma pays in rent which the PIP has assessed as reasonable with regard to the criteria laid down by the ISI. Emma's reasonable living expenses come to €2,071.63.

The PIP will make the following calculation:

Monthly income after income tax and social insurance contributions	€2,600.00
Total set costs	€1,271.63
Rent / mortgage	€300.00
Childcare	€500.00
Special circumstances	None
Reasonable living expenses	€2,071.63
Net disposable income	€528.37

Emma's net disposable income at €528.37 a month is clearly above the €60 limit and on this basis, she is not eligible for a DRN but a DSA may be a possibility.

The PIP, in formulating a proposal to Emma's creditors, might suggest that all of her income in excess of the base level of reasonable living expenses be paid to creditors for year 1. For year 2, as an incentive to keep with the arrangement, the PIP might put forward that Emma retain an additional €25 a month with similar increases in subsequent years.

It will be for creditors to decide if this is acceptable during negotiations with the PIP and ultimately at the point in time that they are asked to vote on the proposal.

Example 2 – Dave and Sarah – DSA

Dave and Sarah are married and have two children. They have a mortgage of €350,000 from Bank A on their family home that is in negative equity and now has a value of €250,000. Dave earns €4,000 per month or €48,000 per annum after tax and Sarah works part time minding children two days a week and earns €500 per month. The combined monthly income after tax is therefore €4,500.

The monthly mortgage repayment on the family home are €2,150 repaying Principal and Interest. The couple have unsecured debts of €40,000 on credit cards, a personal loan from the same bank of €35,000 and a credit union loan of €15,000. The total monthly repayments on the unsecured debts amounts to €800. As with many cases of indebtedness, the couple have started to miss repayments as they have prioritised payments to the credit union and credit card in the belief that they may need to use these in the future. As a result, they are starting to receive a number of legal letters through the post threatening various legal actions to address the mounting arrears.

A DSA will provide the solution. The first stage is to meet a PIP who will review their situation. The couple, quite rightly, would like to leave the family home repayments outside of any arrangement. The DSA will allow the couple to deal with their unsecured debts and so a total of €90,000 will be addressed. The reasonable living expenses guide shows that €1,950 is the applicable total for this family, therefore, after the mortgage repayments, the family has €400 per month to contribute towards an arrangement.

The couple will arrange to transfer this sum per month to the PIP for the term of the DSA who will pay all the unsecured creditors on a pro rata basis. The contributions for the five-year period will total €24,000. The unsecured creditors will therefore receive just over 26% of the outstanding debt. At the end of the five-year period, Dave and Sarah's unsecured debt will be written off. If 65% or more of the unsecured creditors agree to the proposal, it will be passed. In this instance both Bank A and the credit union agree to the proposal.

(Worked examples provided courtesy of the ISI)

6

Personal Insolvency Arrangements

A Personal Insolvency Arrangement (PIA) will allow for the agreed settlement of 'secured debt' up to a level of €3 million, and unsecured debt without any limit. The level of the cap can be increased though, with the consent of all secured creditors, and the length of the agreement will typically be of six years duration.

This type of solution is best suited to someone who has the capacity to pay some of their debts, but is struggling with both secured and unsecured debt problems. This will, crucially, include all of those who are struggling with mortgage debt. As with the DSA, you will need to use the services of a PIP. And again, the first steps will be to prepare the PFS and then for the PIP to secure a Protective Certificate to shield you against your creditors during negotiations.

After this, the PIP will work with you in preparing a proposal for the creditors. For a PIA to be successful, it must be accepted by 65% of all creditors and by at least 50% of both secured and unsecured creditors. In most cases, the banks will have the determining vote, as in the majority of cases the larger percentage of the money owed will be to the banks.

The PIA will involve creating and adhering to a strict budget over a six-year period. The rules for reasonable living expenses will be the same as for the DSA and can be found on the ISI website and also in Appendix 2 at the back of this book. You will not be allowed to enter into a PIA unless at least one of the creditors involved is a secured creditor holding security over an interest in property of yours situated in Ireland. One of the advantages of the PIA is that the proposal that is made to the creditors could include:

- A lump sum payment to creditors
- A payment arrangement with creditors or
- The sale of specified assets under the supervision of the PIP with creditors receiving the proceeds of the sale

It is important to remember that when you have entered a PIA, you cannot transfer, lease, or otherwise dispose of any interest in property above a prescribed value otherwise than in accordance with the terms of the PIA. As with the DSA, it is important that any proposal is both realistic and sustainable if you are going to be able to make it work. If you fall into arrears again and have not made the necessary agreed payments for a period of six months, the PIA is deemed to have failed. This is a situation that nobody wants to occur, least of all the debtor.

Example – Conor – PIA

This example is designed to show how these guidelines are applied in the case of a debtor who is living beyond his or her means.

Conor is employed as an accountant and takes home €4,000 a month. He is single and lives in an apartment which he bought in 2006 for €280,000 but which is now valued at about €160,000. The outstanding mortgage balance is now €258,000 and the monthly payment is €1,200. He also has a mortgage with an outstanding balance of €210,000 on a buy-to-let property which is unoccupied. Conor has a personal loan from a bank with an outstanding balance of €39,000 and outstanding balances totalling €22,000 on three credit cards. He owns outright a car worth €25,000. His discretionary spending leaves him little money to pay his debts. He is hoping that a PIA or DSA can solve his financial problems.

Conor should look at the information on both DSAs and PIAs available on the ISI website before visiting a PIP. He can get a list of PIPs from the ISI website.

Using Table 2 (one adult household, vehicle), the total set costs for the household are €1,029.83 a month. To this is added the €1,200 which Conor pays in mortgage payments which the PIP has assessed as reasonable with regard to the relevant criteria. Conor's reasonable living expenses come to €2,229.83.

The PIP will make the following calculation:

Monthly income after income tax and social insurance contributions	€4,000.00
Total set costs	€1,029.83
Mortgage – reduced payment under the proposal	€1,200.00
Childcare	None
Special circumstances	None
Reasonable living expenses	€2,229.83
Net disposable income	€1,770.17

For Conor's application, this means income of €4,000 minus reasonable living expenses of €2,229.83, giving a net disposable income of €1,770.17 a month.

Conor is living beyond his means. The PIP will likely advise Conor that he will need to consider reducing his spending so as to enable the PIP to put forward a proposal more likely to achieve creditor support while keeping Conor in his home. The PIP, in formulating a proposal to Conor's creditors, will consider Conor's need for a car and may suggest that he should sell his car and either not replace it at all or replace it with a less expensive model.

(Worked example provided courtesy of the ISI)

7

Mediation

There is a saying amongst senior bankers that I utterly failed to grasp during my time at Barings. This is that 'Your first loss is your least loss'. What the phrase means is that things seldom get better once they start to slide, and if you can liquidate your position or your security reasonably quickly, even though you will be taking a financial hit, it is very possibly the best that you are going to do. Essentially, it is the opposite position taken by the gambler who 'doubles down', and hopes to reverse his losses by gambling more. This is as true standing on the trading floor as it is when looking at the state of a property portfolio.

During my own time, I was aware of the fact that I should be cutting my losses at the first opportunity, but I didn't. While my first losses stood at several thousand dollars, the ultimate liability that toppled the bank eventually grew to that colossal figure of £862 million, with disastrous results. The numbers bandied around in financial markets today admittedly dwarf this figure, but the growth in my own starting figure to the point it finally reached is a startling reminder of what can happen if you do not address a problem.

I believe that taking a loss, being prudent when things are taking a turn for the worse, is something that needs to be taught. It is essentially counter-intuitive, strikes at our pride and at the innate sense of unfounded optimism that many of us are inclined towards. No one ever enters a financial transaction expecting it to go wrong.

More often than not, if you're anything like me, you might freeze, like a rabbit in the headlights. You are unable to deal with the immediate situation, but to feel like you are addressing the issue in some way, you might take minor steps, which toy with the issue rather than robustly addressing the underlying problem. In my case I certainly froze. I wasn't able to deal with the problem on my own, but equally was unable to talk to anybody else about it or look for help.

I was ashamed that I was failing and too embarrassed to share my concerns, so I carried on as if nothing was wrong. After faltering through those first initial stages, the problem tends to escalate and you become well and truly stuck. There is no ignoring the situation anymore, but the further it worsens, the more the tendency is to want to avoid dealing with it at all.

I'm sure many distressed borrowers feel similar to how I did, as I waited for that hallelujah moment when the market would rally and fix all my problems. Those type of moments, however, come along very, very rarely, and often not at all. In my case, the Nikkei 225 fell from 40,000 to 18,000, and fell further still after my departure. In the case of Ireland, I feel that it's unlikely that we will see the boomtime levels of residential property prices for decades to come. That may not be a bad thing in itself, as it would suggest that our children have learnt from their parents.

It is also true that many of those who became involved in the housing bubble in Ireland, particularly buy-to-let investors who were seeking a financial return rather than a home, might not have fully understood the fundamentals of their investment decision. Although this is not true for everyone, there were a lot of people in Ireland who bought on the assumption that the house prices would always keep increasing. This was a very risky position to take, and one which was bound to fail if there was any economic downturn or, as sadly turned out to be the case, a global financial crisis of a scale never before seen.

The debt problem in Ireland is almost entirely property related. It is of a scale so large that it feeds into every other problem that exists in the Irish financial spectrum. A massive number of people with mortgages are now unable to make full repayment to the bank as prescribed by the terms of their loan, and the Loan-to-Book values of the homes (the outstanding balance of the loan versus the current market value) are also largely negative. Both of these factors present significant difficulties to the bank. If the numbers of people affected were small, they would be able to cope. They make provisions for a certain percentage of loans to default or become impaired. Faced with the volume of people in difficulty at the moment, however, much like you or I might, they freeze.

The inactivity of the Irish banks which resulted, however, is hard to understand, and I cannot believe that it would occur in any other jurisdiction. As mentioned previously, there are examples of borrowers who have not paid a cent on their mortgage in four or five years. The banks have essentially been frozen.

Now, however, they are starting to thaw, but what remains to be seen is whether this will prove to be a positive thing for borrowers, and for the nation. What I mean by this is that they are now starting to deal with the problems. Files left untouched for years are being dusted off and, in some cases, even opened. It is the start of a process whereby we will begin to see a higher volume of the rebasing of household debt. I refer to this as 'rebasing' rather than 'write-down', as this is a word which can still spook the horses in banking circles, but I have no doubt that through a combination of negotiation and the use of DRNs, DSAs and PIAs a new, acceptable level of debt will be reached. You can call it by whatever name you like, but what it really represents is debt forgiveness in a more palatable guise.

And what did former President Bill Clinton say in November on a visit to Ireland? He said that Ireland will not move forward until there is debt forgiveness. Of course, the Americans are the world leaders in dealing with debt crisis, with an ingrained mentality that failure is not a sin, but something that happens and from which people learn. They have proved the worth of this time and again, and, in the past eighteen months, the US economy has started to come out of recession, unemployment figures are dropping and houses are selling again. And their banks are lending again. The reason for this is that the government was aggressively proactive, which was not the case in Ireland or in many other nations.

But what I would like to talk about now is another avenue worth exploring, outside the formal debt arrangements referred to in the previous chapters.

Negotiation is not the right word in this case as negotiation suggests that both sides have something to give or take; I prefer the word 'mediation'. In this scenario, while a certain amount of sacrifice will be experienced on both sides, the reality is that the brunt of the financial sacrifice to be made will be on the side of the creditor, most likely the bank.

Mediation takes time, as would any negotiation, but the target is to reach the best possible solution for each individual's personal situation. There is no such thing as one size fits all but there are similarities across a number of cases, and I will give examples of some of these shortly. To mediate successfully, the person or institution which undertakes this on behalf of the debtor should have an acute understanding of the market and the stakeholders within it.

As I've already mentioned, the vast majority of debt in this country is property related, and the corollary of this is that a large number of the people whose debts make up this overall figure will have property-related problems. For them, it would make sense to look for a representative that is able to combine real-estate experience with a thorough knowledge of banking, finance and law.

The usual process of the banks is extremely frustrating to the borrower, continually changing policy and staff, pulling you through the mangle one more time so ultimately you go bankrupt. No bank's policy will be to make you go bankrupt but if you yourself do so, it makes their job a whole lot easier. Many give up the ghost. Nowhere is this more apparent than in the type of bankruptcy petitions that are being presented in Northern Ireland at present. Virtually none are creditor petitions, they are all debtor petitions. Some are seeking the finality that comes with being declared bankrupt, others are worn down by the approach of the banks and their apparent inactivity around the situation.

Any proposal to a bank needs to be professionally presented, and should be prepared by somebody who is fully competent in presenting these type of proposals, and perhaps, most importantly, is aware of the current working policies of that particular bank. Due to the fluctuating nature of the financial landscape at the moment, these policies can change frequently, either by their own direction, or by that of the Central Bank, the Troika or the ECB.

In addition, what might be acceptable to one 'pillar bank', might not be acceptable to another, and might be wholly different again to the position that will be taken by an overseas bank.

As is the case with the appointment of a PIP, an element to consider in the appointment of a mediator is to what degree the stress of dealing with your creditors might be lessened. There has been much commentary about the dangers of stress, and they are all too real, so whatever scenario the debtor should choose, this is something that we should all pay careful attention to, and to lessen whenever possible.

There is no doubt, from my experience, that banks ideally prefer to deal with debtors outside of the Insolvency Legislation. The starting position for any bank is that they want to get back all of the money that they are owed, both principal and interest. This is their financial model, and it is hard to argue that they do not have good reason to take this position.

In normal times, or when confronted by a borrower who is able to pay but is choosing not to – the 'strategic defaulters' that are mentioned so frequently – I would think this is to be entirely expected. However, we are not living in normal times, so other avenues should be explored.

As with every other scenario, the starting point is to make sure you have a clear idea of exactly what your financial situation is. This will be necessary for a mediator to propose a solution to your creditors. There might be certain things you are seeking to preserve that are more important than others, and it is these elements that you can discuss, but it is just as important in this route as with the DSA or PIA that whatever plan you choose should be sustainable. In this, it is important that your advisor is able to give you realistic advice.

When I arrived in Hoechst Prison on 1 March 1995, as a newly arrested inmate, one of the first things that struck me was how many innocent people were in prison. Anyone you spoke to would tell you that they were innocent, and how, when they got to court, their lawyer would definitely have them set free. One German kid on my wing had stabbed his girlfriend thirty-seven times, eventually killing her, but every time he was readied to go to court he would move from cell to cell saying his goodbyes and expecting to be granted freedom. A couple of hours later he'd be back, and rightly so. But there were a number of lawyers who, it seemed, were fostering levels of optimism in their clients that I could not understand.

My own lawyer, on the other hand, was the most reasonable, honest and realistic lawyer you could hope to have. When we spoke about my sentence it was never about 'if' I would go to jail, only about 'how long for'. Likewise, he repeatedly described me as the best client he had, as I never expected to be set free. I actually wanted to go to jail as soon as possible, the sooner to get it over and done with. One thing I did want to try and achieve, if possible, was to serve my sentence in the UK, but I was clearly told that this was not something we would be able to control. It was disappointing at the time, but ultimately true. In a scenario where you are seeking the advice and counsel of someone acting on your behalf, you might not like the advice they give you, but it is their responsibility to be realistic with you, for your own benefit. Once you have come to terms with the likely outcomes, it will be far easier to accept them when they come to pass.

It is widely held that there are four concepts of a successful negotiation, and these are as follows:

Best Alternative

It is important that you have considered all the options if you fail to come to an agreement with your lender over your initial proposal. There are always options, so it is important that each of these is considered carefully, and that you have more than one alternative plan.

Areas of Possible Agreement

Your lender and either you or your representative will explore a range of areas where there is common ground, hoping to find a solution. Your lender will want the loan repaid in full, but they will also want to end up with a loan that is being serviced, and without new arrears building up. If you can service a lesser amount, this in itself can provide a possible solution.

Trading Value

Borrowers and lenders will have different aims, so it may be possible to achieve part of your aims whilst compromising on others. It is vital that all the individual areas of the mediation have been discussed with your advisor before the stage of making any formal agreement. This will mean that everyone knows what you are prepared to possibly sacrifice if needed, and the areas in which you would prefer not to move.

Walk Away Position

There will be a point at which you see no value in agreeing to the deal, and both you and your lender will have a 'walk-away' point. Your bank may decide that a sale is the only option and you may feel that bankruptcy now represents a better option for you. Regardless of how much you might want to avoid this choice, you will be better armed in your negotiation, and your planning, if this is also an option that you have reviewed in advance, so you know exactly what this would mean for you.

Part of any planning that leads to mediation must follow certain processes. It is important that you request copies of all the relevant loan documentation and that these are reviewed by a professional to see that they are completed correctly. Recent audits at a number of the larger banks have found that many of the documents are incomplete, have not been signed by all the relevant parties and therefore the security is impaired. During the heady days of the Celtic Tiger, not all documentation was as thorough as it might have been, particularly, ironically, for some of the larger loans, so this is certainly worth checking very carefully. If it is the case that there is any issue, it will drastically alter for the better your negotiating stance with the bank.

Case 1 – Mediation, Full and Final Settlement

The client involved was a large player in the leisure industry who was facing difficult times and experiencing a slow-down in business that necessitated a restructuring. As with a number of businesses at the moment, he had purchased property and those property loans were now in considerable negative equity. Whilst the client had been negotiating with the bank for the last couple of years, they had come to the conclusion that they were getting nowhere fast. The total value of the loans was €5.1 million and the current asset value in 2012 was only €2 million.

A group of independent advisors were appointed to act on the behalf of the borrower as he was convinced that bankruptcy was his only option. The advisors sought to mediate with the bank and make a proposal that was of benefit to both parties. In order to achieve this, the proposal had to be as robust as possible. After months of negotiation, the advisors agreed on behalf of the borrower to sell the underlying assets to the loans through a consensual sale process. The banks prefer this method of disposal as it removes the need to appoint an official receiver to the property which increases costs and has a significant adverse effect on the market value of the assets. The advisors managed this process, providing an effective buffer to the client, dealing directly with the bank and added value to both bank and borrower.

The advisor had successfully negotiated that the residential property of the borrower was excluded from any informal arrangement. A shortfall of €3.1 million was crystalized after the sale of assets but the client had achieved his main target of remaining in his private primary residence. A contribution of €100,000 was offered by the borrower to settle the shortfall and this was split between all lenders. As the client had been open, willing and transparent throughout the process and had engaged effectively, the bank was willing to accept that this was the extent of his ability to pay. The client was obviously delighted that this situation had been solved but the bank was also happy that they had achieved a better return than they would have had they appointed a receiver.

Case Two – Existing Trading Business and Property Company

The client had two limited companies, one which was a property development company, the other was not. The property company was struggling but the other company was trading well and was unaffected by the property crash. The property company had two different lenders who were looking for solutions from the borrower, who was at a loss how to move forward and achieve the result that he was looking for. He had been negotiating himself with the bank and receiving help from his company accountant but both were becoming frustrated with the fact that they were achieving nothing. The accountant was finding the bank very difficult to deal with.

The accountant employed a firm of advisors to find a solution. The debt was a total of €1.4 million and the value of the assets had slumped to €600,000, so a shortfall in the region of €800,000. The client had provided personal guarantees to the two lenders, one for €350,000, the other for €250,000. With the agreement of the banks, the advisors sold the two properties and crystalized the shortfall. The advisors managed the sale of assets and added value to the net return of the disposal process.

In the discovery process of reviewing the loan documentation and the security review it became apparent that some of the documentation had not been signed correctly.

The impairment of the paperwork allowed the advisors to target a more favourable solution for the borrower. As they became aware of the difficulties, the banks became eager to find a quick solution and also wanted a solution outside of any formal insolvency process. The banks had little wriggle room due to the professional manner in which the detail was collected and subsequently presented.

The non-property company was excluded from the arrangement and this therefore provided a future income stream for the client. The banks avoided any protracted legal cases over the impaired security and loan documentation and were prepared to accept that this was the best possible solution that they could arrive at. The debt in the property company was settled at 25 cents in the euro and the client was delighted that he had retained control over one of his companies so that he could look forward to the future.

Case 3 – Restructure of Existing Facilities

In this case, the client had just received a facility renewal letter from the lender. The relationship between bank and borrower had not been going well and there was a certain amount of tension building up between the client and the Relationship Manager at the bank. This is often found to be the case as the Relationship Manager is changed on a regular basis and you often find yourself explaining the situation time and time again to someone new. In this case the client was now with his third Relationship Manger in eighteen months. This may be a deliberate tactic of the banks or evidence of the fact that staff working in these areas become disillusioned, demoralised and sometimes face just as much stress as the borrower.

The client had a number of trading businesses which were doing ok but the new facility letter was looking for a monthly repayment of €10,000 per month, an increase of two thirds from his previous repayment of €6,000 per month. This would have been completely unsustainable. The client thought he had little alternative but to place the businesses into liquidation. His accountant was failing to present the case succinctly to the bank and was equally unsure of their policy and afraid to rock the boat.

Advisors were appointed to mediate with the bank. An Independent Business review was the first stage of this and the findings were presented to the bank along with an indication of the client's ability to pay. After several months of negotiation, a new facility letter was drawn up and it was agreed that the client would now pay €4,500 per month. The advisors persuaded the bank that this was the best solution and that the other possible connotations would result in a significantly lower return to the bank. Again the client was delighted as he had saved on fees associated with any more dramatic course of action, his businesses were still trading and he had made considerable savings on his interest payments.

Case 4 – Buy-to-Lets with Family Home

The client had six buy-to-let properties of which five were in negative equity and one was at par value. The client also had his principal private residence upon which he had a mortgage of €300,000 but now only had a market value of €250,000. The client had always been open, willing and transparent with the banks but was now in a situation whereby he was unable to pay the mortgage as it stood. He did not have the skillset to deal with the banks successfully and, like many others, felt that he was going round in circles and achieving very little.

He was overly stressed with the situation and needed a solution. He engaged a group of advisors to negotiate with the banks on his behalf. Understanding the process far better than he ever had before, the stress started to lift. The client had two different lenders. Having made a presentation to the banks, the client received a more favourable rate on his mortgage which was in line with his ability to pay. Any loan, after all, has to be based on affordability. The advisor agreed to the consensual sale of the buy-to-let properties and six months later crystallised a loss of €150,000. The client worked aggressively through the sale process to achieve the best return for the banks. It was not a distressed sale and the bank had no costs relating to receivers, so they were happy with the outcome. The client was able to offer a lump sum payment of €20,000 which was split between both lenders and which was accepted as settlement. Common sense had prevailed.

The important thing to remember is that every case has a solution. In the current financial environment that we now live in, the banks are now often willingly engaging in many of the processes outlined above to try and resolve the chronic debt problems on a case-by-case basis.

8

Bankruptcy

A number of respected personal finance journalists and market commentators have suggested that the new bankruptcy rules in Ireland strike the right balance. In truth, I really do not think they can be further from the mark. The rule makers are still very much in the mindset that any insolvency measures must punish rather than provide a pathway to a new start. For me, this is exactly the wrong attitude and raises the question of how many people will actually avail of the opportunities that the new legislation provides.

Until now, Irish bankruptcy legislation was among the most archaic in the world, effectively condemning the bankrupt to a lifetime of penury in an economic wasteland. All that an Irish bankrupt had to look forward to was a miserable existence where he or she could retain the tools of their trade but very little else. Any prospective earnings were the subject of attachment orders on behalf of their creditors, and there was little, if any, incentive for the bankrupt to trade their way back to financial stability. Planning for the future was impossible and the original debt was often sustained by the requirement to reimburse the petitioner's legal costs.

The old laws insisted upon a twelve-year discharge period from bankruptcy, which is an incredibly long time to wander around with no real purpose, regardless of the size of the debt. Whilst this approach was one that was inherited from the UK, the UK model was overhauled over two decades ago, while Ireland's remained the same. We have effectively been using some of our most outdated laws to handle a very new scale of problem, and this has caused issues.

Early research suggested that the rate of applications for bankruptcy under the new legislation would be huge. With an estimate of 6,900 cases for year one, the rate was predicted to be well ahead of those in England, Wales and Northern Ireland. By historical levels this would be a very significant increase but I find it hard to believe this will come to pass, because of the aspects of the legislation which still remain punitive.

Bankruptcy essentially has a dual purpose. This is to protect the creditors, firstly, but also to make it possible for someone in difficulty to finally draw a line under a bad situation and move forward. Under the new rules, discharge now becomes automatic at the end of the third year of the process. This is certainly a positive development, but when you add in the fact that there is a twelve-month qualifying period beforehand, and the very real possibility of a further five years of claw-back on your earnings afterwards, the widespread relief at the news that there was going to be a change in the legislation was short-lived. And the problem is that, if we are not creating an option which is workable for many, they will look for alternative routes, be that burying their head in the sand, or looking overseas ...

This is what has been referred to as 'bankruptcy tourism', and it has become a common theme in a number of the leading publications, particularly as there have been a number of high-profile applicants of late. Some of the articles are written in such a way that the author appears to be surprised that people might still want to do this, when new legislation is coming into place. In fact, I have listened to many financial experts in the Irish media over the past few months, and it seems that there might not be enough clarity about this legislation. Moreover, it seems very obvious that the new legislation will do little to stem the race across the Irish Sea, or even the Atlantic.

After studying the new rules, there is a real sense that the voice of the banks and the large accountancy practices can be clearly heard in the documentation. Aside from the length of time before automatic discharge being three years, the new bankruptcy law will bar you from being a director in a company for three years and if you have any chance of making any financial success in the near future, there may be a five-year claw back. Take the scenario whereby you have a pretty ambitious young entrepreneur who has a number of buy-to-let properties as a result of boomtime investments, but also a good SME business with lots of potential. After studying the new legislation, trying to work out what his best options would be, some things become immediately clear: if he stays in Ireland, there is a good chance it may take him eight or nine years to deal with his debt; if he decides to go to the UK, it will be twelve months. Where is that guy going to want to resolve his debt problem?

There is a good chance some of those people will look at the option of moving to England or up to Northern Ireland for a number of years, as they are not prepared to put their life on hold – and it is hard to argue with this thinking. It is a problem for the country as a whole, since the apparent lack of progressive change seems to be driving people out of the country itself.

Externally, Ireland is being held up as an example of a country overcoming problems and successfully administering austerity. Internally, many people are still facing quite severe difficulties and, for some, there is a significant lack of hope. Tourism bankruptcy will continue to be a very real choice for some and, to be quite honest, there is very little anyone can do about it. It is unfortunate that the government didn't duplicate (or design something that resembles) the insolvency legislation that works well in the UK, as this might have addressed this problem directly.

The recent high-profile bankruptcy applications that have been made in foreign jurisdictions such as the US and the UK have done little to promote the institution of bankruptcy to either the general public or the banks. The man in the street might, understandably, come to the conclusion that the deeper you are in debt and the more reckless your behaviour has been, the greater the capacity you have to avail of the softer offers elsewhere. The banks, possibly correctly in a number of cases, perceive the borrower to be hiding assets from them and not being as transparent as they should be. These high-profile bankruptcy cases muddy the waters with their actions, and can lead the bank to start any form of negotiation with the preconception that the debtor is hiding something from them. This is generally not the case but everyone is becoming tarred with the same brush. The contrast between the fortunes of the high-profile developer bankrupt and the individual who overpaid for a family home before losing their livelihood could not be starker. It is most definitely unfair that it seems to be the most indebted who are the ones to take advantage of the softer overseas regimes, but that is the way that it is at present. As with so many things financial, it is often those who most need to take advantage of all the possible avenues that are least aware of how to find them.

For many people looking for the quickest way out of serious levels of debt, the UK has now become a more realistic option. Property developers and celebrities are not the only people heading to Britain to avail of its more lenient insolvency laws; many everyday people are making the short journey across the Irish Sea. Informed observers suggest that this number is increasing steadily, and that the new legislation has actually accelerated this trend. The process simply seems to be most things that the Irish system is not; and that is lenient, simple and fast. The completion of a couple of forms and one trip to a county court sees you making the first steps to a new start, as under EU law, EU citizens can legally declare bankruptcy in another member state, as long as they can prove that their centre of main interest is in their new country, and they have rescinded links with their home nation.

The process is as valid as any other, but it is clearly open to abuse. The point upon which a number of the high-profile attempts to be declared bankrupt in the UK have rightly failed has related to whether or not the person has truly severed links with Ireland. Quite appropriately, when this happens, the banks have taken a very hard line in protecting their interests. The Bank of Ireland, for one, successfully challenged an application that was brought by a customer by clearly showing that their links with Ireland remained very strong. The Irish Bank Resolution Corporation (IBRC) fought a client's attempts to be declared bankrupt in Belfast and successfully forced the process to go through Dublin instead, as it proved that the Republic remained his centre of main interest. In short, the judges have become far more concerned about how permanent a move really is.

Quite simply, if you move and stay, you are entitled to the order. If you are not working and cannot demonstrate that you have moved completely to the new jurisdiction, the process is open to challenge. In the majority of cases there is not the same level of dispute with the banks as there have been in those cases that have hit the headlines. While they may not receive the same amount of scrutiny from their creditors, they will rightly come under scrutiny from the court, so it is important that their application is not frivolous. Judges are obviously very keen to witness the correct degree of permanency in the move, as well as looking at future intentions and evidence that you will be living in the state for a period after the hearing. In short, the move must have a degree of permanency about it.

For those availing of this route, they will typically find a place to live in the UK. After this, they will need a National Insurance number, which allows you to look for work or work on a self-employed basis. As with moving to any jurisdiction, they would then need to open a bank account and register for utilities such as electricity and gas which will ultimately be used to verify that they are truly resident in the UK.

Once a person can be described as habitually resident, they then contact the local county court and the court will send out an individual bankruptcy pack, which includes a petition and a statement of affairs that need to be completed. The debtor then attends court with three copies of the documentation, as well as the court fee, which also serves as part of the official receivers deposit. After the court has processed the papers, the debtor appears before a judge, who must be satisfied that they are entitled to bankruptcy and that they have established Britain as their centre of main interest. If the judge is satisfied, a bankruptcy order will be granted.

It is at this point that the debtor's affairs will be handled by an official receiver who will get in touch within twenty-four hours of the declared bankruptcy. Within three weeks the receiver will conduct an interview about the statement of affairs provided, before contacting all creditors and realising any assets that may be for their benefit. If there are no unforeseen circumstances, the bankruptcy will come to an end automatically in twelve months' time.

Everyone will have a different opinion on the validity or morality of such an approach.

If it can be proved that the process is being manipulated and abused, it should quite rightly be challenged and overturned.

It is one of many options for the individual to consider for themselves, and make up their own mind, but it is not an avenue that should be necessarily closed. I can see why people might seek to avoid a regime they see as unduly punitive, when what they actually want is the chance of a clean slate, and the possibility to improve their economic prospects and those of their family. I struggle to find fault if that is the genuine purpose. The rights and wrongs of the UK and US insolvency regimes can be debated all day long, and no doubt they will be, but the overriding fact is that both of them have been shown to work, and to deliver the borrower to a stage whereby he can start again. This provides the incentive that everyone is looking for.

It is in this area, that of incentive, that we have been let down most significantly by the new legislation. The most important objective of bankruptcy law is to promote sufficient repayment from debtors so that lenders will be willing to continue lending to other borrowers. Without the sanction of bankruptcy, the incentive for banks to lend is diminished and everybody suffers. If that happens, consumption will become entirely linked to income, and there will be nothing to smooth out the curve during times of economic downturn. The interests of the creditor and the bank need to be addressed, both need motivation. The sanctions have weighed heavily against the borrower in the past and the new legislation has done little to alter that. Economic recovery will only come after a line has been drawn under the debt problems in this country. In many respects, the American ethos, whereby the bankrupt sacrifices their unprotected assets but future earnings are protected, means that bankrupts have a fresh start and are heavily incentivised to work hard and earn. There is just no such incentive in the Irish legislation.

There are other important objectives, however, in any bankruptcy law, which are worth looking at. One of these is that creditors must be prevented from seriously harming debtors and other creditors by aggressively positioning themselves to be the first to collect, once it has become clear that a debtor is in serious financial distress. Certain actions by those creditors can lead to the debtor being unable to make best use of assets, and examples of these are as follows:

- Repossessing equipment that may affect the debtors potential earnings
- Consolidating loans and converting them from unsecured to secured debts
- Seizing a disproportionate amount of any income/assets thereby damaging the interests of other creditors

There are examples of this happening already, with unsecured creditors looking to collect what they can to the detriment of those that have security in place.

The most important objective of any bankruptcy regime is to prevent long-term damage, both personal and economic. It is in nobody's interest, as a nation, to have medical issues going untreated, or to have children leaving school early because their parents are unable to pay for their education. These have a knock-on effect that we would all suffer from, both individually and as a nation. Bankruptcy should be primarily about seeking to avoid anything that might create a dangerous downward spiral in the future.

Banks do not often have much to gain from making their clients bankrupt as it serves no real purpose unless they have exhausted all other avenues. But, if you fail to engage with them and try to reach a workable solution, they are sometimes left with no other option. As painful as it may be to take a step in the right direction, it is important this happens. It is necessary to pull back the veneer of what everybody normally sees and expose the real problems that lie underneath. I know I am not a shining light in this regard, but my experience of this did not end well. The constant battle between my worry and pride on one side, and the dawning reality on the other led me to crumble from within.

Many people treat this kind of problem in a similar vein. Keeping up appearances in social circles remains important. It is something which, to varying degrees, affects us all, but in these matters can obviously become quite damaging. Aside from the growing financial problems, the underlying stress that it can create can sometimes be a greater concern in itself.

I would say, however, that personally I feel bankruptcy is always the last option. In the vast majority of cases I would simply not consider it, and is only something to look at after all viable alternatives have been exhausted. To put it in perspective, I lost £862 million and never went bankrupt; the banks lost substantially more than this, many billions, and a solution was found; large multi-nationals often restructure their debt to allow themselves to move on and fight another day. In none of these instances was the protagonist forced into bankruptcy. Therefore why should you be? However, this does not alter the fact that it is an absolute necessity to have an effective domestic bankruptcy regime and, in turn, how that effective regime contributes to the smooth working of the economy.

9

Mortgages

The type of loan that is causing the biggest headache for the government today clearly remains mortgage debt. That is why the resolution of the mortgage arrears is receiving so much attention at the moment, coupled with the fact that the Troika are actively looking for progression in dealing with the arrears before Ireland exits the bailout programe at the end of 2013.

We live in a society where everyone traditionally had a desire to own their own home. There was talk that this was 'in our genes', which was nonsense, but there was certainly a culture of home-ownership, fostered by the lack of protection afforded to those who might have otherwise rented, in comparison to other European nations. We also had no shortage of land, we are not over-populated, and above all, we had a property boom in which many people who might not have done so otherwise, committed themselves to mort-gages they could not really afford for fear that they would soon be utterly priced out of the market. This is a road well-travelled and does not require much more discussion here since we all know how the story ended.

Missed mortgage payments are generally a clear symptom of underlying personal financial distress. Chronic loan delinquency can ruin a person's credit history and, in the most extreme of cases, can lead to repossession of your home. As a nation, mass repossessions, even in theory, are hard to accept, with their echoes of our darker colonial past. The psychological shift in accepting that they have the potential to become a real possibility is still underway.

An individual arrears case at a bank will raise very few eyebrows. It has always been a consequence of lending money that a small per-centage of people will be unable to repay that money in full. For as long as there has been lending, there have been bad debts, but when the scale of arrears grows larger, even by a few per cent, it becomes a very serious problem at an institutional level. Widespread missed payments rapidly eat away at the profitability of a bank, reducing its capital reserves, and can ultimately threaten its very existence. So when you have a situation like the one we are facing now, where one in eight borrowers cannot pay back their loans on time or in full, the whole banking system is essentially in jeopardy.

Figures released by the Central Bank for the first three months of 2013 reported that 95,554 residential mortgage accounts for the family home were now in arrears of at least ninety days. That accounted for more than 12% of the total stock of loans, and reflected a marked increase from only three months earlier, and an increase of 3,205 from the figure at the end of 2012. When you add in more than 29,000 buy-to-let mortgages that are suffering the same fate, there were at least 124,000 home loans that were in trouble. The total value of those non-performing loans stands at over €20 billion. These figures do not include the 59,000 or so 'early arrears cases' where fewer than three payments have been missed and a further 55,000 mortgage cases that have been restructured and are technically no longer in arrears, but cannot be considered performing in the traditional sense of the word. It does not take a mathematician to conclude that one in four mortgages in Ireland is actually, therefore, a problem loan to some degree.

Figures for the first three months of 2013 also showed that 142,118 households were behind with mortgage repayments. Of these 25,940 had been in arrears for over two years, which was a staggering 12% jump quarter on quarter, clear evidence that the problem is accelerating rather than decelerating. The most unfortunate statistic was that 166 homes were repossessed between January and March of 2013. For a nation unused to the extremity of this measure, this number shows the real and present threat of the consequence of not paying a mortgage.

Every missed or partial payment represents lost money to a bank, and the equivalent sum has to be subtracted from income. Worse still, as soon as the arrears pass the ninety days past due date, the loan becomes classified as impaired and the value of the loan has to be marked down. When this happens, further bank capital has to be allocated against further losses. Whilst this represents the direct financial cost of large-scale arrears, perhaps the most damaging cost to borrower and lender is the administrative challenges that lenders have when dealing with them. It is a momentous challenge, which the banks were not entirely geared up for. Arrears or collections departments are typically small in size, as the number of errant loans was only ever a small percentage of the total. With one in four loans now causing problems, staff originally employed to acquire customers, service accounts or sell new products have to be redeployed to manage arrears. Not all are suited to the role and new staff have to be hired, or the role farmed out to a third party, both of which bring additional cost to the bank, depleting their profit margins further. In the banks' opinion, the opportunity cost is probably the most significant, as, rather than making money, they are forced to focus on trying to recover it.

The pressure is coming from a number of sources to deal with the arrears problem. The Central Bank, the Department of Finance and the Troika all want to see the issue resolved. The first step along this path came when the Central Bank instructed lenders to produce loan modification programmes that would address the simpler cases. To stress the need for immediate action, the regulators imposed more onerous rules on recognising impairments and provisioning for those same loans. This simply meant that, if you did not address the impaired loans and reach a solution, more loans would count as arrears and the damage to the balance sheet would become greater. Long overdue, 2012 saw a significant change in this direction from the regulators. Lenders were castigated by Fiona Muldoon, the Central Bank's head of credit institutions and insurance, for not dealing with the arrears issue more robustly. If they did not face up to the nature and scale of the arrears problem and take action, she warned them that the regulators would. Now, rather than allowing the banks time to solve the problem in their preferred way, the Central Bank wanted action. If the arrears question is not dealt with, it would ultimately necessitate another taxpayer bailout, and this was to be avoided at all cost. Whether this will yet happen remains to be seen, but it is not a scenario that anyone wants.

The banks, however, have two huge incentives to act. The first of these is that the Central Bank could force mortgage lenders to provide for a 100% loss on their loans if they do not meet quantitative targets for restructuring them, which would damaging their balance sheet further. New personal insolvency legislation will bring other creditors to the fore, and banks would not want to surrender control of how a delinquent loan is managed to any other party. The threat of an insolvency application, as a result, may well prove more influential in trying to strike a balance and a restructuring with your bank. Mortgage borrowers will not be able to avail of insolvency arrangements unless they have already entered into the mortgage arrears resolution process with their bank.

The subject of mortgage debt draws many different responses, depending on who you are talking to. The banks in Ireland would simply not be able to withstand wholesale default on behalf of their borrowers. Neither are they able to offer widespread write-down across the spectrum of mortgage classes, despite what people might want, as both cases would result in the banks becoming insolvent. That is what represents the moral hazard facing those with the decision-making capability.

The most common concern that we see amongst banks is how to differentiate between those borrowers who can't pay and those that won't pay. Differentiating between the two classes takes up a lot of time and distracts from the real purpose of finding workable solutions. It can often be a difficult distinction, and the consequences of getting it wrong are significant. It is referred to in the media as a 'strategic default', and while it only concerns a small minority of debtors, the fact that it is happening is causing delays and adding a level of complexity and confusion to the issue. If a debtor is exposed as attempting to take this position, they should not expect to be treated with kid gloves.

Thankfully, the vast majority of those in trouble are honestly trying to engage with their banks. I have no doubt that an element of debt forgiveness is inevitable at some stage, but it should only happen for those that are open, willing and transparent. As I cannot stress enough, communicating with your bank is the first vital step towards finding a solution. Those who fail to engage with their bank will always be afforded less protection.

The Central Bank set out a code of conduct on mortgage arrears, which requires lenders to establish a Mortgage Arrears Resolution Process (MARP) and use it when dealing with customers who are in arrears, or those who believe they are in danger of falling into arrears. The MARP has five stages:

- Effective communication
- Gathering financial information
- Assessment of the borrowers situation
- Finding a solution to the problem
- An appeal option for those who remain dissatisfied

Those going through this process will be required to fill in a detailed form called a Standard Financial Statement (SFS). This will provide a comprehensive overview of your situation and will be used as the basis for negotiating a settlement. Unfortunately, no bank has a menu of solutions that you can review, with a view to choosing the one that you feel is most appropriate. In many cases, you will find that the bank is looking for you to provide the solution, or at least to propose an arrangement that they can review and assess. 'Forbearance' and 'restructuring' are the most common phrases that are bandied about but there is no guarantee that these are readily available to you. Your lender will want to look at each case on its individual merits and assure themselves that the solution proposed is both achievable and sustainable. Many borrowers find this part of the process confusing, as they are unable to understand the banks' approach and have no idea how they themselves can formulate a proposal. This is when sound independent financial advice can prove invaluable, and it should be sought whenever possible. The clear objective of MARP, as it is for the insolvency legislation, is to find a solution that does not involve the sale of the family home.

To date, the banks' initial approach to resolving debt issues has been forbearance. This is generally a short-term option, and might result in an interest-only period, an extension of the mortgage term, or in some cases a 'payment holiday'. As the extent of the mortgage arrears started to really become apparent, however, the banks have shifted away from these options, to those which are more creative and long-term in nature. The options available now have spread out to include 'split mortgages', 'negative-equity trade downs', 'mortgage-to-rent' schemes and the consensual sale of property to maximise the return and minimise shortfall. A word of caution though: when the words 'creative' and 'banks' are included in the same sentence, it is wise to be careful. Amongst their list of recent creative developments are 'endowment mortgages', 'sub-prime debt' and 'credit default swaps', all of which have now been consigned to a desolate financial graveyard. In any dealings with the bank, it is worth remembering that the bank will (generally) long outlive you, so you might not always have the same perspective on time. It is important to get all the details of any potential arrangement, and that you scrutinise this very carefully. A phrase that I have come across more regularly of late is the notion that a bank might 'give you your day in your home', meaning they will allow you to live there until you pass away and then they will assume ownership. Unless no other resolution is at all possible, you should be setting your sights higher.

A split-mortgage involves a portion of the outstanding loan being 'parked', or set-aside for a number of years, to give the struggling borrower breathing space. I will give you an example of this at the end of this chapter. A 'trade-down mortgage' is relatively straight-forward, and would see a borrower selling their negative-equity home and purchasing a new property at a lower price. Different banks are offering different variations of these deals. For example, some banks charge interest on the 'parked' portion of the split mortgage, and others do not. Last month, the government and the Central Bank unveiled a new plan that impressed upon the banks the need to agree workable solutions with indebted borrowers. The Central Bank has told the banks that at least half of their customers whose mortgages are in arrears must be offered sustainable solutions before the year is out, otherwise the bank may face hefty penalties that will form a significant restriction on their business. Unfortunately, the decision on what constitutes a 'sustainable solution' rests with the bank. The official line from the banks remains that debts will not be written off. Having said that, if a person goes down the route of personal insolvency, a proportion of their debts will be have to be written off, so effectively, nothing is entirely off the table.

Borrowers in distress do have access to a free independent professional consultation with an accountant, who can talk them through the implications of any proposal that a lender has put to them. The lender, in this instance, pays the fee on behalf of the distressed borrower.

There is little doubt that repossessions will become far more frequent now, as a loophole which previously prevented lenders from taking this route has now been closed. The Central Bank have publicly stated that they expect the level of repossessions to rise from the current levels, though they do also remain positive that, where borrowers are cooperating with their lenders, they can expect that repossession will be the absolute last resort and will only be used in cases where there is no valid and sustainable long-term solution.

There is, however, some good news for buy-to-let mortgage holders. If you have an investment property and have fallen behind with your mortgage, your case will not fall under the code of conduct on mortgage arrears, which is currently limited to the treatment of the family home. While this can mean that a more flexible solution is a possibility, the targets set for lenders in relation to the number of sustainable solutions also includes buy-to-let investors, so a solution of some sort will have to be found.

In all cases, the first step to a solution is through communicating and engaging with your lender. This might not happen immediately, as the banks have their own problems to overcome, in that the staff dealing with arrears are often overwhelmed by the sheer volume of cases that they face. A MABS report revealed that many borrowers are waiting in excess of two months for a response from lenders to their correspondence.

Debt is an emotional subject and that is true for lender to some degree as well. It should not be forgotten that the person you might be dealing with in your bank might well have similar problems of their own. Add to that the fact that the resolution process can be drawn out and emotionally testing for both parties, and it might be easier to see how it can be difficult to strike a balance between what is strategically correct for the bank and what is morally required for the borrower. The process is far from easy, so everyone should be prepared for that, but that certainly does not mean that a good solution cannot be found.

One example of a possible solution mentioned earlier was the split-mortgage option, and an example of this is below:

Split Mortgage through a Personal Insolvency Arrangement

John is 40 and works as an accountant in Dublin. His salary is €90,000 per annum or €4,700 per month after tax. Five years ago John and his wife Jill bought the family home for €400,000 and the house is now valued at €300,000. The mortgage outstanding on the property is €350,000 from Bank A and monthly principal and interest repayments stand at €2,120. They have two young children under the age of 5, and Jill has given up her job to stay at home and look after the children. They also own one other property which they bought as an investment, which cost €300,000 but is now valued at €150,000. Unfortunately, the property is not let as they have been unable to secure tenants.

John and Jill have also amassed credit card debts of €25,000 and a bank loan from a separate bank, Bank B of €35,000. As in a lot of cases, this additional loan was undertaken to assist with their daily living expenses. The monthly cost associated with servicing these unsecured loans is €650. The couple have no savings but are due an inheritance of €25,000 from Jill's late mother.The couple reviewed the ISI website and have attended a meeting with a PIP to assess what solutions are available to then.

The PIP will assess the reasonable living expenses to be €2,150.

He may make the following proposal:

- That the family be allowed reasonable living expenses of €2,250 per month
- That the mortgage of €350,000 be split (€200,000 being paid as principal and interest at a rate of €1,265 per month and the balance of €150,000 being placed on interest only for the term of the PIA and then revert to Principal and Interest. The monthly repayment for the term of the PIA will be €500
- That the investment property be sold for its market value of €180,000 with the shortfall of €120,000 being treated as unsecured
- That €685 per month be paid to the unsecured creditors (€4,700 less €2,250

reasonable living expenses, less €1,765
mortgage payments)
· That on receipt of the €25,000 inheritance monies, it immediately be paid to
the unsecured creditors

Based on the proposal, the unsecured creditors
will receive €74,000 over the six-year term of
the arrangement, including the inheritance sum.
This equates to about 41% of the unsecured
debts outstanding.

It remains the case that 65% of the overall
creditors must agree the proposal and at least
50% of the secured and unsecured lenders. In this
case, Bank A will control the overall voting.

At the end of the arrangement, John and Jill
will be in a position to pay the full Principal
and Interest repayments on their mortgage for
the remaining years of that mortgage. Their
overall cash liquidity will improve enormously
at the completion of the process.

There is a Code of Conduct on Mortgage
Arrears that was issued under Section 117 of
the Central Bank Act 1989. It must be remem-
bered that it only applies to your primary
residence but sets out a set of criteria by which
the mortgage lenders must treat the borrowers facing mortgage arrears. In particular the
act clearly demonstrates that each case of

mortgage arrears is unique and needs to be considered on its own merits. The code sets out the framework that lenders must work within when dealing with borrowers. All such cases must be handled sympathetically and positively by the lender with the objective at all times of assisting the borrower in meeting his/her mortgage obligations.

For definition, arrears arise on a mortgage loan account where a borrower has not made a full mortgage repayment or only makes a partial repayment, as per the original mortgage contract by the scheduled due date. A borrower can also be considered a pre-arrears case whereby they contact the lender to inform them that they are in danger of going into financial difficulties and are concerned about going into arrears on their mortgage payments. The code is designed to allow you the space and time to find a resolution whilst allowing you to remain in your own home. As with all of the measures that we are discussing, it is important that you know and follow the Code of Conduct on Mortgage Arrears as it represents your key protection in the case of financial difficulties with your house.

The process will seek to achieve a number of key targets:

- That you are treated fairly by your lender
- The process is the same for all borrowers and is transparent
- The lender must explain clearly your options for rescheduling your loan
- The lender must stick to any new agreement, provided that you do too

(Worked example provided courtesy of the ISI)

10

Where Do We Go From Here?

My wife is a nervous flyer. I am not. When the flight takes off she will grab the seat, or my arm, while I use the flight as a time to relax, sleep and catch up on things that I need to do. Because of the nature of my work, I have flown extensively over the years, much of it long-haul, and I have encountered most of the bad weather that aircraft have to face. I've boarded planes at Hong Kong airport only a couple of hours after there had been an accident, and, on one occasion, many of the injured were sitting on the new plane when I took my seat. My philosophy is quite simple. The pilot has a particularly vested interest in getting you to your destination safely, that being his own life, so I have no problem in handing over complete control.

The only other profession that receives my almost total confidence is that of a surgeon. I have been under the surgeon's knife once or twice in the past and may well be again in the future, but as with a pilot, their interest is in saving lives and looking after your safety. I still like to ask questions, though, and to fully understand their processes and their responses to my questions as much as possible.

Banks do not have the same sort of vested interest in your welfare. Regardless of their intentions, it is a numbers game. They try their best, and some are clearly better than others, but at the end of the day, it is a business. They are looking to sell a product and, like any other salesperson, the more they sell, the better they do and the higher the bonus. It's not personal, and it would be wrong to think they are all mercenaries, but their duty of care, as we have seen over recent years, does not extend very far.

Since the crisis, regulation has been revamped and supervisors have become more hands-on, sitting in on internal bank committee meetings to monitor important decisions. The cosy relationship between the regulator and the banks has been replaced by more critical oversight.

That is a highly positive development. But change is never seamless, and the criticism from within the banks is that the controls have now become more over-bearing and critical challenges to the business are often over-looked. I understand both sides of the argument.

The general public still have great reason to feel aggrieved. Some bankers are doing very little to help themselves, and reluctance of former bankers to give up parts of pensions and other entitlements that were inflated by the boom is not helping the perception. Little individual remorse has been shown for monumental failures of the past.

Unlike certain sectors of the general public, whose ire is understandable, I'm not in favour of the wholesale approach to getting rid of bankers, but the culture definitely requires major changes. Without that, we will only be treading water until the next problem. There should be no second album from the people behind The Anglo Tapes.

But neither should we tar everyone with the same brush. While there may not be too much individual remorse on show, the banks are trying hard to turn the tide and have accepted that action is required. Permanent TSB has acknowledged that there will have to be some debt forgiveness. At the bank's AGM on 22 May,

Permanent TSB CEO Jeremy Masding acknowledged that there will be an element of debt forgiveness for beleaguered borrowers in cases where mortgages cannot be put on a sustainable basis, but this will be on a case-by-case basis, and only after the appropriate period of engagement. He also stated that the bank has been working through their arrears backlog. Masding understandably declined to give details of any cases where debt forgiveness has been granted to date. The bank had 21,131 owner-occupier mortgages over ninety days in-arrears at the end of 2012, and has revealed that standard financial statements had been completed by 11,400 of these in the first four months of the year, with 9,200 of them in some form of forbearance arrangement. This includes split mortgages, where an element of the mortgage has been parked, in the manner referred to earlier.

In contrast, Allied Irish Bank CEO, David Duffy, has suggested that the take-up of its split mortgage offers has been slow – less than 30% of over 1,400 offers have been accepted – as customers have been waiting to see if the personal insolvency legislation was going to provide them with a better option. He has now admitted that there has been an element of write-down on a number of their non-performing loans. On the buy-to-let side, over 5,000

PTSB cases were over ninety days in-arrears at the end of 2012, and the bank has reportedly dealt with around half of these, with 800 now in a forbearance arrangement.

In its AGM statement, the bank set out its three major priorities: to restructure the business to create a viable competitive banking force for the Irish marketplace; to work closely with customers in arrears to help them manage their challenges; and to use capital efficiently in the management of 'non-core' portfolios. The bank is back and competing for mortgage business, car loans, educational loans and current accounts. New lending activity in 2012 was only €0.1 billion, as the focus was on managing arrears and the development of new lending strategies which will be implemented in the current year. The bank plans 'to approve lending of up to nine times more this year than in 2012'. It has taken in over €500 million of customer funds so far this year. They are clearly making the right noises.

The domestic banks are undergoing their biggest restructuring since the formation of Bank of Ireland and AIB a half-century ago as the government attempts to repair balance sheets, purge the banks of unprofitable loans and recover some of the €64 billion of State cash that was injected into the Irish financial institutions. There were six indigenous lenders a year ago. Now there are four. The former Educational Building Society has been reversed into AIB. Anglo Irish Bank has taken over Irish Nationwide Building Society and been renamed Irish Bank Resolution Corporation (IBRC), and was then wound down. Permanent TSB is being separated from its profitable life assurance business, Irish Life, which had, until last year, saved the bank assurance group from government control. A good bank of about €14 billion in loans or 'New Permanent TSB' is being carved out of the mess to create what the Minister for Finance Michael Noonan believes could become a third national banking force to compete against two so-called 'pillar' banks of Bank of Ireland and AIB.

We shall see what happens. There is definitely a need for other lenders on these shores, but there are not too many institutions beating down the door. Bank of Scotland, Lloyds and Danske will likely never return; huge losses mean they have been severely bitten and have become shy as a result. The fate of Ulster Bank also seems uncertain. They are aggressively unloading property, along with their own flagship premises and may well be formalising an exit from Ireland very shortly.

Bank of Ireland is the only domestic bank to remain outside the controlling hands of the government after taking in €1.1 billion of North American private investment last year in return for a 35% stake, reducing the State's interest to 15%. The lender is also the only Irish bank to retain a presence on the main Irish stock market, as the tiny sliver of shares still held by the crash-weary shareholders at AIB and Permanent TSB moved to the junior Dublin market, the Enterprise Securities Market, which allowed the two lenders to avoid Anglo's fate of outright nationalisation. It is worth noting that one aspect of Bank of Ireland's approach was to ask one of their most-respected elder statesmen, Pat Molloy, who had run the bank in a very different and more conservative age, to return to the fold for a time, and the bank has now seemingly steered itself to safer waters once again.

All of the Irish banks are slimming down from their bloated boom-years size. They are selling loans and other excess assets to bring their loans closer in line with deposits that stayed in the Irish system. They are about halfway to their target loans-to-deposit ratio of 122.5%, the level which was set by the Central Bank as sustainable. This will reduce their over-reliance on the ECB from which they had borrowed €65 billion at the end of March 2012.

The bulk of the loans that have been taken out of the banks have arisen over the past two years as a result of the transfers to the National Asset Management Agency (NAMA), the government body set up to purge the banks of their most toxic loans, mostly in the area of property development. This has removed €74 billion of loans from the balance sheets of the Irish banks. Beyond that, the banks had been downsizing radically by shedding loan books and businesses. Including the loan transfers to NAMA, Bank of Ireland has reduced its loan book by €42 billion since 2008, AIB by €44 billion and the former Anglo Irish Bank by €55 billion.

This reduction has, however, meant a sharp decrease in the number of staff in Irish banking. The Irish Bank Officials Association (IBOA) has estimated that about 6,000 employees have left Irish banking since the financial crash of 2008 and more departures are to come with 2,500 at AIB and 1,000 at Bank of Ireland (as estimated by the IBOA but unconfirmed by the bank). Combined staff numbers at what were previously Anglo Irish Bank and Irish Nationwide fell from more than 2,000 to 1,200 staff at the end of 2011, followed by sharp reductions in 2012, followed by the rapid, indeed overnight, liquidation. The once mighty AIB, now effectively nationalised, following the receipt of €20 billion in government hand-outs, employs about 15,000 staff, down from close to 26,000 at the peak of the boom when it still had businesses in Poland and the US.

There are about 30,000 people working in retail banking in Ireland at the moment, down from 35,000 in 2009, according to the Irish Banking Federation, while it says there are about 33,000 in international financial services where employment numbers have held up pretty well, despite the global nature of the financial crisis. The foreign retail banks are not immune from the strain of the banking crash. Ulster Bank is aggressively working through problem loans and cutting almost 1,000 jobs. Bank of Scotland (Ireland) is being run down by Lloyds subsidiary Bank of Scotland through Certus, a company run by members of the former management team at the Irish bank. National Irish Bank is being merged with Northern Bank in Northern Ireland and the NIB name will be removed from over the doors of its Irish branches. Dutch group Rabobank is working through heavy losses at ACC Bank, while KBC Bank Ireland is being supported by its parent bank in Belgium to cover higher loan losses.

The nature of financial regulation played no small part in the Irish banking crisis and it's still not clear whether the new regulator's risk-based approach will make Ireland less competitive and attractive as a financial centre, as compared with rivals in Europe and further afield. International firms point to the need to maintain credible regulation and to avoid the kind of regulatory arbitrage or weak supervision that tends to lumps Ireland in with weakly-regulated centres.

Risk is something that we all live with on a daily basis. We all have to make assessments of where we have to assume risk, where we seek to mitigate or minimise that risk, or else simply become risk averse. In market talk these are simply described as 'risk on: risk off'. That's fine when you have control over your own finances but, as we have seen, the financial markets continue to present constant danger of overheating. So the real question must be, where is the next risk coming from?

The latest reports from the credit rating agency Fitch suggests that China's shadow banking system is now out of control, and that it is coming under increasing stress as borrowers struggle to roll over and repay short term debts. Sound familiar? The scale of credit and lending in China is said to be so extreme that the country will find it very hard to grow its way out of the excesses as they have done in the past. This can only lead to tougher times ahead. China has enjoyed fantastic growth through a credit-driven model that is now in very real danger of falling apart. This could then materialise into a massive over-capacity problem that could lead to a Japanese-style deflation. Systemic risk is rising and there is a lack of transparency in their banking system, so it is difficult to see who the lenders and borrowers are, and to evaluate properly the quality of the assets that underpin many of the loans. At the moment, their banks look to be in good shape with non-performing loans at a low level, but trusts, wealth management funds and off-shore vehicles are responsible for half of the new credit being supplied. This would suggest that there is a question mark over whether any bad assets are being moved around to paint a better picture. The suggestion is that a lot of the banking exposure to property is not being reflected as well as it might, which, if true, would represent very real risk.

So, the message is that we are not out of the wood yet, but you personally can be. I do have some criticism of the new legislation around personal debt, as I have mentioned, particularly around bankruptcy. Britain reduced their period of discharge from ten years to three some decades ago, and in 2004 they reduced this further, from three to one. In Ireland, it feels as if the change was forced upon the government, and, as a result, was not as whole-hearted as it otherwise might have been. I still feel that it retains a punitive aspect which I struggle to agree with.

But, the new insolvency legislation in this country can work. Rebasing household debt through the three vehicles of DRN, DSA and PIA can achieve the required results, if creditors and banks work together to accept the arrangements. The Central Bank and Regulator has a huge role to play in ensuring that this happens.

The purpose in writing this book was twofold; firstly, to make it clear that you are not on your own, there are many people in a similar, if not worse situation; secondly, to try and show you that there is always a manageable solution. It does not need to be as overwhelming or indeed as desperate as many people may sometimes feel. Earlier this year, *Stubbs Gazette* published some of the first research into the likely take-up of personal insolvency schemes in Ireland. The results showed very clearly a country with massive pent-up demand for debt relief, even though most of the people surveyed were unaware of what form that this may take. Some estimates suggested that a staggering quarter of a million households would qualify for one of the three schemes on offer. And personally, I think these figures are underestimated. So, it is worth noting that the neighbour that people might be struggling to keep up with might very well be in the same boat as you, and may actually need your shoulder as much as you might need theirs. This is no longer an issue to feel ashamed of. If you were alone in this, to put it in perspective, it is unlikely that there would be so much debate.

Ideally, I would like to think that even in some small way, you might feel more empowered by this stage. Educated is too strong a word, people are well versed, and I know my limitations, but I'd like to think you might be more aware of some of your options, and in a better position to ask the right questions. We must all continue to question everything, as too many people with responsibility have had it far too easy for far too long. Taking back control of your finances has never been as important as it is today.

Many years ago, when I was sat at a trading desk in Singapore, life was good. I had just arrived, enjoying the life of an expat, with money in my pocket. There was no limit to what I thought I could achieve, and I was always trying to push that horizon further. I was 25 years old and thought I could cope with anything. I was mistaken, and the next few years taught me that lesson very clearly. I could have done one thing very differently though; I could have asked for help and advice. Had I sought that, my story would have been very different. As much as I hate and am embarrassed by what happened in that dark period, I believe that we are all the sum of our experiences and that part of my life has contributed to what I am today. As much as you might struggle with your money problems, and as overwhelming as they might well seem, I can assure you there is a way through them. But always look for help and advice. You are certainly not alone.

Recently, the G8 visited Northern Ireland, where they stayed in a world class hotel. This hotel is currently run by the receivers. On their next visit to these shores, wouldn't it be fantastic if that same hotel was owned and controlled by an Irish hotelier? That would be progress.

List of Abbreviations

AI   Approved Intermediary
AIB   Allied Irish Banks
CVA   Company Voluntary Arrangements
DRN   Debt Relief Notice
DSA   Debt Settlement Arrangement
ECB   European Central Bank
IBOA   Irish Bank Officials Association
IBRC   Irish Bank Resolution Corporation
INBS   Irish Nationwide Building Society
ISEQ   Irish Stock Exchange Quotient
ISI   Insolvency Service of Ireland
IVA   Individual Voluntary Arrangements
LRC   Law Reform Commission
MABS   Money Advice and Budgeting Service
MARP   Mortgage Arrears Resolution Process
NAMA   National Asset Management Agency

PFS	Prescribed Financial Statement
PIA	Personal Insolvency Arrangement
PIP	Personal Insolvency Practitioner
SFS	Standard Financial Statement

Useful Sources of Information

Aware support services, www.aware.ie

Citizens Information Board, www.citizensin-formation.ie

Insolvency Service of Ireland, www.isi.gov.ie

www.keepingyourhome.ie

Money Advice and Budgeting Service, www.mabs.ie

National Consumer Agency, www.nca.ie/your-money

Vincentian Partnership for Social Justice, www.vpsi.ie

The author's websites, www.nickleeson.com and www.gdpni.com

Tables for the Calculation of Reasonable Living Expenses

Table 1:
One-Adult Household, No Vehicle

Monthly total set costs €933.14

Other Costs
Housing
Special circumstances
Reasonable living expenses

Set cost breakdown –
For illustrative purposes only:

Food	€250.98
Clothing	€35.34
Personal Care	€33.06
Health	€31.34
Household Goods	€26.38
Household Services	€27.54
Communications	€41.21
Social Inclusion & Participation	€126.10
Education	€23.72
Transport (Public)	€149.70
Household Electricity	€60.37
Home Heating	€70.80
Personal Costs	€0.97
Home Insurance	€12.25
Car Insurance	€0.00
Savings and Contingencies	€43.38
Total Monthly Set Costs	**€933.14**

Table 2:
One-Adult Household, Vehicle

Monthly total set costs € 1,045.48

Other Costs
Housing
Special circumstances
Reasonable living expenses

Set cost breakdown –
For illustrative purposes only:

Food	€250.98
Clothing	€35.34
Personal Care	€33.06
Health	€31.34
Household Goods	€26.38
Household Services	€27.54
Communications	€41.21
Social Inclusion & Participation	€126.10
Education	€23.72
Transport (Private)	€237.79
Household Electricity	€60.37
Home Heating	€70.80
Personal Costs	€0.97
Home Insurance	€12.25
Car Insurance	€24.25
Savings and Contingencies	€43.38
Total Monthly Set Costs	**€1,045.48**

Table 3:
One-Adult Household, One or More Children, No Vehicle

	Adult	Child Age Groups				Adjustment if more than two children	
		Infant	Pre-School	Primary	Secondary	Third Child	Fourth Child
Total before deductions	€939.71	€372.26	€208.52	€349.37	€562.16	€10.81	€10.27
LESS child benefit	*€0.00*	*-€130.00*	*-€130.00*	*-€130.00*	*-€130.00*	*€0.00*	*-€10.00*
Total Set Costs	€939.71	€242.26	€78.52	€219.37	€432.16	€10.81	€0.27

Other Costs
Childcare
Housing
Special circumstances
Reasonable living expenses

Set cost breakdown –
For illustrative purposes only:

	Adult	Infant	Pre-School	Primary	Secondary
		Child Age Groups			
Food	€222.51	€135.44	€105.11	€162.43	€215.88
Clothing	€35.33	€71.99	€21.86	€29.90	€54.44
Personal Care	€31.40	€46.51	€6.09	€11.74	€36.43
Health	€29.20	€35.98	€18.85	€18.60	€24.50
Household Goods	€62.37	€45.58	€11.78	€13.17	€16.04
Household Services	€27.54	€0.00	€0.00	€0.00	€0.00
Communications	€41.07	€0.00	€0.00	€0.00	€20.48
Social Inclusion & Participation	€99.31	€7.72	€10.04	€49.58	€93.33
Education	€10.34	€0.00	€0.00	€29.16	€66.27
Transport (Public)	€125.00	€0.00	€12.25	€12.25	€12.25
Household Electricity	€86.08	€6.30	€0.00	€0.00	€0.00
Home Heating	€91.45	€0.00	€0.00	€0.00	€0.00
Personal Costs	€0.95	€1.05	€0.85	€0.85	€0.85
Home Insurance	€17.59	€0.00	€0.00	€0.00	€0.00
Car Insurance	€0.00	€0.00	€0.00	€0.00	€0.00
Savings & Contingencies	€59.57	€21.69	€21.69	€21.69	€21.69
Total Before Deductions	€939.71	€372.26	€208.52	€349.37	€562.16
LESS Child Benefit	€0.00	-€130.00	-€130.00	-€130.00	-€130.00
Total Monthly Set Costs	€939.71	€242.26	€78.52	€219.37	€432.16

Table 4:
One-Adult Household, One or More Children, Vehicle

		Child Age Groups				Adjustment if more than two children	
	Adult	Infant	Pre-School	Primary	Secondary	Third Child	Fourth Child
Total before deductions	€1,091.15	€372.26	€196.27	€337.12	€549.91	€10.81	€52.72
LESS child benefit	*€0.00*	*-€130.00*	*-€130.00*	*-€130.00*	*-€130.00*	*€0.00*	*-€10.00*
Total Set Costs	€1,091.15	€242.26	€66.27	€207.12	€419.91	€10.81	€42.72

Other Costs
Childcare
Housing
Special circumstances
Reasonable living expenses

Set cost breakdown –
For illustrative purposes only:

		Child Age Groups			
	Adult	Infant	Pre-School	Primary	Secondary
Food	€222.51	€135.44	€105.11	€162.43	€215.88
Clothing	€35.33	€71.99	€21.86	€29.90	€54.44
Personal Care	€31.40	€46.51	€6.09	€11.74	€36.43
Health	€29.20	€35.98	€18.85	€18.60	€24.50
Household Goods	€62.37	€45.58	€11.78	€13.17	€16.04
Household Services	€27.54	€0.00	€0.00	€0.00	€0.00
Communications	€41.07	€0.00	€0.00	€0.00	€20.48
Social Inclusion & Participation	€99.31	€7.72	€10.04	€49.58	€93.33
Education	€10.34	€0.00	€0.00	€29.16	€66.27
Transport (Private)	€250.04	€0.00	€0.00	€0.00	€0.00
Household Electricity	€86.08	€6.30	€0.00	€0.00	€0.00
Home Heating	€91.45	€0.00	€0.00	€0.00	€0.00
Personal Costs	€0.95	€1.05	€0.85	€0.85	€0.85
Home Insurance	€17.59	€0.00	€0.00	€0.00	€0.00
Car Insurance	€26.40	€0.00	€0.00	€0.00	€0.00
Savings & Contingencies	€59.57	€21.69	€21.69	€21.69	€21.69
Total Before Deductions	€1,091.15	€372.26	€196.27	€337.12	€549.91
LESS Child Benefit	€0.00	-€130.00	-€130.000	-€130.00	-€130.00
Total Monthly Set Costs	€1,091.15	€242.26	€66.27	€207.12	€419.91

Table 5:
Two-Adult Household, One or More Children, No Vehicle

	Couple	Infant	Pre-School	Primary	Secondary	Third Child	Fourth Child
		Child Age Groups				Adjustment if more than two children	
Total before deductions	€1,360.30	€372.26	€208.52	€349.37	€562.16	€10.81	€10.27
LESS child benefit	*€0.00*	*-€130.00*	*-€130.00*	*-€130.00*	*-€130.00*	*€0.00*	*-€10.00*
Total Set Costs	€1,360.30	€242.26	€78.52	€219.37	€432.16	€10.81	€0.27

Other Costs
Childcare
Housing
Special Circumstances
Reasonable Living Expenses

Set cost breakdown –
For illustrative purposes only:

| | Child Age Groups | | | | |
	Couple	Infant	Pre-School	Primary	Secondary
Food	€283.21	€135.44	€105.11	€162.43	€215.88
Clothing	€66.73	€71.99	€21.86	€29.90	€54.44
Personal Care	€64.90	€46.51	€6.09	€11.74	€36.43
Health	€45.17	€35.98	€18.85	€18.60	€24.50
Household Goods	€67.63	€45.58	€11.78	€13.17	€16.04
Household Services	€27.54	€0.00	€0.00	€0.00	€0.00
Communications	€61.56	€0.00	€0.00	€0.00	€20.48
Social Inclusion & Participation	€158.02	€7.72	€10.04	€49.58	€93.33
Education	€10.34	€0.00	€0.00	€29.16	€66.37
Transport (Public)	€250.00	€0.00	€12.25	€12.25	€12.25
Household Electricity	€112.39	€6.30	€0.00	€0.00	€0.00
Home Heating	€114.46	€0.00	€0.00	€0.00	€0.00
Personal Costs	€1.91	€1.05	€0.85	€0.85	€0.85
Home Insurance	€17.59	€0.00	€0.00	€0.00	€0.00
Car Insurance	€0.00	€0.00	€0.00	€0.00	€0.00
Savings & Contingencies	€78.85	€21.69	€21.69	€21.69	€21.69
Total Before Deductions	€1,360.30	€372.26	€208.52	€349.37	€562.16
LESS Child Benefit	*€0.00*	*-€130.00*	*-€130.00*	*-€130.00*	*-€130.00*
Total Monthly Set Costs	**€1360.30**	**€242.26**	**€78.52**	**€219.37**	**€432.16**

Table 6:
Two-Adult Household, One or More Children, Vehicle

		Child Age Groups				Adjustment if more than two children	
	Couple	Infant	Pre-School	Primary	Secondary	Third Child	Fourth Child
Total before deductions	€1,407.50	€372.26	€196.27	€337.12	€549.91	€10.81	€52.72
LESS child benefit	€0.00	-€130.00	-€130.00	-€130.00	-€130.00	€0.00	-€10.00
Total Set Costs	€1,407.50	€242.26	€66.27	€207.12	€419.91	€10.81	€42.72

Other Costs
Childcare
Housing
Special Circumstances
Reasonable Living Expenses

Set cost breakdown –
For illustrative purposes only:

	Couple	Infant	Pre-School	Primary	Secondary
		Child Age Groups			
Food	€283.21	€135.44	€105.11	€162.43	€215.88
Clothing	€66.73	€71.99	€21.86	€29.90	€54.44
Personal Care	€64.90	€46.51	€6.09	€11.74	€36.43
Health	€45.17	€35.98	€18.85	€18.60	€24.50
Household Goods	€67.63	€45.58	€11.78	€13.17	€16.04
Household Services	€27.54	€0.00	€0.00	€0.00	€0.00
Communications	€61.56	€0.00	€0.00	€0.00	€20.48
Social Inclusion & Participation	€158.02	€7.72	€10.04	€49.58	€93.33
Education	€10.34	€0.00	€0.00	€29.16	€66.27
Transport (Private)	€250.50	€0.00	€0.00	€0.00	€0.00
Household Electricity	€112.39	€6.30	€0.00	€0.00	€0.00
Home Heating	€114.46	€0.00	€0.00	€0.00	€0.00
Personal Costs	€1.91	€1.05	€0.85	€0.85	€0.85
Home Insurance	€17.59	€0.00	€0.00	€0.00	€0.00
Car Insurance	€46.70	€0.00	€0.00	€0.00	€0.00
Savings & Contingencies	€78.85	€21.69	€21.69	€21.69	€21.69
Total Before Deductions	€1,407.50	€372.26	€196.27	€337.12	€549.91
LESS Child Benefit	€0.00	-€130.00	-€130.00	-€130.00	-€130.00
Total Monthly Set Costs	**€1,407.50**	**€242.26**	**€66.27**	**€207.12**	**€419.91**